NEW YORK CITY

|CONDENSED|

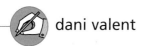 dani valent

LONELY PLANET PUBLICATIONS
Melbourne • Oakland • London • Paris

contents

New York City Condensed
2nd edition – February 2002
First published – April 2000

Published by
Lonely Planet Publications Pty Ltd
ABN 36 005 607 983
90 Maribyrnong St, Footscray, Vic 3011, Australia
www.lonelyplanet.com or AOL keyword: lp

Lonely Planet offices
Australia Locked Bag 1, Footscray, Vic 3011
☎ 613 8379 8000 fax 613 8379 8111
e talk2us@lonelyplanet.com.au
USA   150 Linden St, Oakland, CA 94607
☎ 510 893 8555 Toll Free: 800 275 8555
fax 510 893 8572
e info@lonelyplanet.com
UK   10a Spring Place, London NW5 3BH
☎ 020 7428 4800 fax 020 7428 4828
e go@lonelyplanet.co.uk
France   1 rue du Dahomey, 75011 Paris
☎ 01 55 25 33 00 fax 01 55 25 33 01
e bip@lonelyplanet.fr
www.lonelyplanet.fr

Design Emily Douglas Maps Gina Gillich, Bart Wright and
Annette Olson Editing Valerie Sinzdak, Tom Downs and
Emily Wolman Cover Daniel New Publishing Manager
Diana Saad Thanks to Gabrielle Green, James Hardy,
Charles Rawlings-Way, Ruth Askevold, Annie Horner,
Kerrie Williams, Susan Rimerman, Kate Hoffman, Mariah
Bear, Susan Derby, John Spelman and Caroline Mardok.

Photographs
Many of the images in this guide are available for
licensing from Lonely Planet Images.
e lpi@lonelyplanet.com.au;
www.lonelyplanetimages.com
Images also used with kind permission of
Frick Collection, New York and The Metropolitan
Museum of Art, © Bill Melton, Wild Bill Studios

Front cover photographs
Top: Evening, Lower Manhattan
(Angus Oborn)
Bottom: Statue of Liberty
(Angus Oborn)

ISBN 1 86450 250 9

Text & maps © Lonely Planet Publications 2002
Manhattan Subway map © Metropolitan
Transportation Authority (used with permission)
Photos © photographers as indicated 2002
Printed through Colorcraft Ltd, Hong Kong
Printed in China

how to use this book

SYMBOLS

⊠ address

☎ telephone number

⊕ nearest subway station

⊠ nearest train station

⊟ nearest bus route

⊟ auto route, parking details

⊘ opening hours

ⓘ tourist information

⑨ cost, entry charge

e email/website address

♿ wheelchair access

⚱ child-friendly

✖ onsite or nearby eatery

V good vegetarian selection

COLOR-CODING

Each chapter has a different color code, which is reflected on the maps for quick reference (eg, all Highlights are bright yellow on the maps).

MAPS

The fold-out maps inside front and back covers are numbered from 1 to 6. All sights and venues in the text have map references that indicate where to find them on the maps; eg, (3, G4) means Map 3, grid reference G4. Although each item is not pin-pointed on the maps, the street address is always indicated.

PRICES

Price gradings (eg $10/5) usually indicate adult/concession entry charges to a venue. Concession prices can include senior, student, member or coupon discounts.

AUTHOR AUTHOR!

Dani Valent

During an eight-year association with Lonely Planet, Dani Valent has worked on a dozen travel guides to destinations on four continents. New York has drawn her back time and again with its spirit, pace and gutsy humor. If she didn't have to get home to feed the dog in Melbourne, Australia, she'd be eating bagels and shaking some booty in New York 12 months of the year.

Thanks to Braden King, Beth Dixson, Mia Dentoni, Allison Jurjens and Eva White.

READER FEEDBACK

Things change – prices go up, schedules change, good places go bad and bad places improve or go bankrupt. So, if you find things better or worse, recently opened or long since closed, please tell us and help make the next edition even more accurate. Send all correspondence to the Lonely Planet office closest to you (listed on p. 2) or visit www.lonelyplanet.com/feedback.

facts about new york city

New York is exhilarating, resilient, spirited – it's bursting with spectacle and possibility and hope. At any given moment – now, now and now! – the city is expressing itself. A guy's flossing his teeth on the subway, a waiter's writing a novel in the library and a dame is shopping Madison Ave with a parrot on her shoulder. There's a constant chatter: people are talking to one another, throwing unsolicited commentary your way ('hey, I like your shirt') or singing for anyone who's listening. Inanimate objects want to be heard, too. There's the hum of machines and buildings, the hymn of taxis and trains. Even the street signs speak up, declaring, 'Don't even *think* about parking here.' It's New York, it's abuzz, and there's nowhere to match it in the world.

New York is a feast of humans being everything they can be: good, bad, funny, friendly and indifferent. They're engaging in spontaneous raps, getting the toddler off to analysis or appearing from nowhere with umbrellas to peddle in a rainstorm. Whether you're selling lobster bisque from a hot dog stand or doing the funky chicken in Central Park, no one will bat an eye. Time and time again, Manhattanites refuse to be baffled; the answer to just about anything is a shrugged 'this is New York.'

New Yorkers hail from all over the globe, from Teaneck to Timbuktu, and, like them, you can pursue any dream you want to here. It's not easy – this city is expensive, it's relentless and it's still shell-shocked from the 2001 terrorist attacks. At its best, though, New York is the most intoxicating, energizing metropolis we've got. Be warned – many visitors find it very hard to leave!

Jon Davison

The Chrysler Building (left) stands out in the New York sky.

HISTORY

Native Americans occupied the area now known as New York City for more than 11,000 years – the name 'Manhattan' came from local Munsee Indian words. The first recorded European visitor was Giovanni da Verrazano, in 1524, but Henry Hudson was the first to claim the land for his sponsors, the Dutch East India Company, in 1609.

Colonial Era

The Dutch established their first trading post, Nieuw Amsterdam, in 1624, consolidating their claim two years later by buying Manhattan Island from the Indians for the reputedly small sum of 60 guilders' ($24) worth of gifts.

In 1647, Peter Stuyvesant came to impose order on the unruly colony, but his intolerant religious views led to unrest. Few resisted the 1664 bloodless takeover by the British, who renamed the colony New York.

Minor opposition to British colonial rule developed, but many New Yorkers resisted a war for independence. In fact, New York became a British stronghold. George III's forces controlled the city for most of the American Revolution.

Brooklyn's historic brownstones

Boom Years

George Washington was sworn in as the republic's first president in New York in 1789, but the founding fathers disliked the city, then a bustling and dirty seaport of 33,000 people: Thomas Jefferson described it as 'a cloacina of all the depravities of human nature.' Still, plenty of others liked it: by 1830, the population had exploded to 250,000.

Manhattan's distinctive street grid was imposed by the Planning Commission in 1811, and in 1842 the Croton Aqueduct brought freshwater to improve public health. Commerce and infrastructure boomed.

Growing Pains

New York's explosive growth continued in the late 19th century. Corrupt politicians milked millions from public-works projects, while industrial barons amassed tax-free fortunes. The poorest New Yorkers worked in dangerous factories and lived in squalid tenements.

The severely limited space in the downtown business district meant the only way to go was up, and by the late 19th century Manhattan had a cluster of new multistory buildings called 'skyscrapers.' An expanding network of subways and elevated trains made the city's outer reaches accessible, and in 1898 the growing, independent districts of Queens, Staten Island, the Bronx and Brooklyn became 'boroughs' of a consolidated New York City.

With another wave of European immigrants, the population of the new metropolis leapt from three million in 1900 to seven million in 1930. The Depression caused enormous distress, but Mayor Fiorello La Guardia expanded the social service network.

Decline & Renewal

After WWII, New York became the world's premier city, but it soon suffered from middle-class flight to the suburbs. Television production, manufacturing and even the fabled Brooklyn Dodgers baseball team moved to the West Coast. By the 1970s, only a massive federal loan program rescued the city from bankruptcy. Led by colorful three-term mayor Ed Koch, New York regained much of its swagger in the 1980s. The city, though periodically divided by racial conflict, elected its first African American mayor, David Dinkins, in 1989. After a disappointing single term, he was ousted by the city's overwhelmingly Democratic voters (a cruel irony) and replaced with Republican Rudy Giuliani. In two terms that polarized residents, Giuliani clamped down on crime, enabling the controversial sprucing up of Times Square, the East Village and Harlem.

> **Incoming...**
> 'I support a very specific type of immigration control. I think we should only let people born in other countries get into New York.' – Humorist Fran Lebowitz

New York City Today

Though saddened and sobered by the terrorist attacks on the World Trade Center on September 11, 2001, New York has responded with a characteristic combination of civic pride and community spirit. Amid the distress and jitters, this remains a chaotically thriving city.

ORIENTATION

New York City sits at the mouth of the Hudson River where it meets the west end of Long Island Sound. The city, actually made up of some 50 islands with 309 sq miles (800 sq km) land mass, comprises five boroughs: the Bronx, Brooklyn, Manhattan, Queens and Staten Island.

Most of Manhattan (population 1.5 million) is easy to navigate, thanks to a grid system of avenues running north-south, cut across by numbered streets that run east-west. Navigation is trickier south of 14th St, as streets snake along haphazardly. Above Washington Square, 5th Ave serves as the dividing line between the East Side and the West Side.

The Bronx (population 1.2 million) is the most northerly borough and the only one on the mainland. Brooklyn, on the western tip of Long Island, is the most populous of the outer boroughs, with 2.3 million people. Queens, adjoining Brooklyn on Long Island, is the largest and most ethnically diverse borough in the city, with some two million people speaking 120 languages. Staten Island (population 443,000), southwest of Brooklyn, can be reached by the famous and free Staten Island Ferry.

ENVIRONMENT

New York has come a long way in improving air and waterway quality, but the city's streets are anything but pristine, and its infrastructure is in desperate need of improvement. Summer heat taxes electricity supply and causes brownouts (brief power outages), and heavy rain can shut down the subways; sometimes it seems as though the operational veneer of the city is a very thin skin indeed.

Recycling efforts remain patchy and unnecessary consumption rife; the city produces over 26,400,000lbs (11,880,000kg) of waste daily. But, like the city itself, nature has been making a comeback: the opening of a sewage treatment plant on the Upper West Side in 1986 has turned the Hudson River from a dumping ground into a scenic spot again, and harbor seals have been spotted in the East River.

City hall's lawns abloom in spring

GOVERNMENT & POLITICS

New York has a long record of voting for the Democratic Party, though there are conservative pockets in the blue-collar sections of Queens and Brooklyn and throughout suburban Staten Island. Despite the Democratic tradition, socially liberal Republican reformers can be elected mayor, as proved by Rudolph Giuliani.

Many communities boast local activists: childcare, soup kitchens and community gardens are just a few of the resident-run projects that keep the city feeling neighborly.

The city's political structure includes five borough presidents, a city-wide comptroller and a public advocate. New York also has a city council made up of 51 elected officials who represent individual neighborhoods. They're supposed to provide a check on mayoral power, but they've been criticized for lack of political input.

Republican media mogul (and political newcomer) Michael Bloomberg won the mayoral election in late 2001 and took the helm of a city still reeling from one of the most tragic events in New York history.

ECONOMY

New York's fortunes suffered enormously from the World Trade Center disaster, which battered an already faltering economy. Federal aid has mitigated the losses, but they have nevertheless leaked into just about every ledger in the city.

Still, New York could stand alone as its own city state. A major player in the worlds of finance, tourism, and media, it's a prestigious address for major US corporations and most prominent foreign concerns.

Did You Know?

- There are 8 million New Yorkers.
- Over 37 million people visit annually.
- NYC has 70,000 hotel rooms.
- Tourists support 280,000 jobs.
- A tiny studio apartment in Manhattan can cost $1500 a month.
- Annual average income in NYC is $50,000 ($20,000 more than the US average).
- More than 200 feature films are shot in NYC each year.

SOCIETY & CULTURE

New York is a singular example of racial diversity – about 30% of residents are foreign-born, buttressing the city's reputation as the nation's 'melting pot.' Downtown, Asians and Italians have given distinctive personalities to Chinatown and Little Italy, Hispanic communities have settled in the East Village and southern Harlem, and African Americans remain the dominant group in Harlem proper. Washington Heights has drawn immigrants from the Dominican Republic and El Salvador.

Many other ethnic groups have dispersed to the boroughs. Most of the Jewish population, once in the Lower East Side, has moved to the Bronx, Brooklyn and Queens, though the Upper West Side remains strongly Jewish. Koreans have made their homes in Flushing, and Ecuadorians and Colombians have settled in Queens (also home to a large Greek colony in Astoria).

Despite intermittent flarings of racial tension, New York is one of the USA's best-integrated cities. This isn't to say it's one big happy family (it isn't), but millions of New Yorkers of all backgrounds live in close proximity, usually without incident.

Etiquette

There isn't any particular look you can adopt to fit in – practically anything goes, unless you're intending to dine in a fine restaurant (where jacket and tie are required) or a leather bar (BYO whip). The best pose is confidence – you really can do *anything* in this town.

Even the hippest tourist can be marked as an outsider in many tiny ways – by actually looking up at the buildings or attempting to read the *New York Times* on a packed subway without first folding it lengthwise and then in half.

Smoking Smoking cigarettes is as fashionable as farting on the subway. Cancer sticks are banned in government buildings, offices, concert venues, theaters, taxis and public transportation. Cigarettes are not allowed in most restaurants, though you can puff proud in most clubs and bars.

ARTS

Dance

New York has incubated most of the USA's prominent dance companies and choreographers, including Martha Graham. Russian-born choreographer George Balanchine founded the New York City Ballet (now directed by Peter Martins). The Alvin Ailey, Martha Graham and Paul Taylor companies and the Dance Theater of Harlem perform annually.

Film

Martin Scorsese has brought the dark side of the city to life, while Woody Allen continually discovers its comic side. Spike Lee's feature films have exposed the city's racial tensions. Hollywood's A-list actors usually keep a residence here, as well as on the West Coast; Robert de Niro and Gwyneth Paltrow are among those who call New York home.

Literature

New York City's literary scene has nurtured the talents of F Scott Fitzgerald, Henry James, Edith Wharton, Jay McInerney and Tom Wolfe. Current New York–based writers include Pulitzer Prize–winner Michael Cunningham and Australian Peter Carey. For an overview of the city in literature, pick up Shaun O'Connell's *Remarkable, Unspeakable, New York*, a look at how American writers have regarded the country's biggest metropolis over two centuries.

Music

New York is home to some of the foremost classical music and operatic organizations in the world, and leading composers and conductors, including Gustav Mahler, Arturo Toscanini, Leonard Bernstein and John Cage, have achieved fame and fortune here.

Ragtime, a favorite genre in the early 20th century, owed its popularity to Scott Joplin and Irving Berlin. Jazz hit the mainstream in New York thanks to George Gershwin and Duke Ellington. Trumpeter Dizzy Gillespie and saxophonist Charlie Parker ushered in bebop, which gave way to the freer expressions of Miles Davis and Sonny Rollins. Wynton Marsalis and Joshua Redman now lead the way. John Zorn is at the forefront of experimental improv.

Rock-music icons like Bob Dylan, Jim Morrison and Jimi Hendrix found crowds of fans in New York. Of the upcoming young bands, look out for The Strokes.

Painting

Edward Hopper is one of the best-known painters associated with New York. Others include impressionists Childe Hassam and Mary Cassatt, dadaist Marcel Duchamp and abstract expressionists Jackson Pollock and Willem de Kooning. Pop artist Andy Warhol still looms large in the New York art pantheon, as does Jean-Michel Basquiat, a Warhol crewmember who reveled in – and was battered by – the excess and hype of the 1980s.

Photography

Influential figures associated with New York include Alfred Stieglitz and Man Ray, both of whom helped turn photography into an art form, plus such notables as Richard Avedon, Annie Liebowitz, Herb Ritts and prominent photojournalists Margaret Bourke-White and Alfred Eisenstaedt.

Theater

Broadway has hosted the work of most prestigious American playwrights, including Eugene O'Neill, Sam Shepard, August Wilson, David Mamet, Neil Simon and Arthur Miller. Tin Pan Alley composers George Gershwin and Cole Porter produced many of the most enduring musicals. Such is the allure of New York's stages that George M Cohan (theater producer, actor and playwright) said, 'When you are away from old Broadway, you are only camping out.'

Today, Broadway means the large Times Square theaters, which are dominated by overblown spectaculars. 'Off-Broadway' refers to shows in smaller spaces (200 seats or fewer) elsewhere in town. 'Off-off-Broadway' events are fringe or experimental pieces in spaces with fewer than 100 seats.

Times Square: vibrant heart of the theater world

highlights

It's not very 'New York' to race around sightseeing – many residents have never been to the Statue of Liberty and only distantly remember a childhood trip to the Met. Quintessential New York experiences are often chance encounters with locals: loitering in cafés, enjoying impromptu jam sessions in the subway or watching pick-up basketball on a local court.

That said, the highlight attractions here are all world-class: postcard sights are breathtaking, museums and galleries are mind-boggling and some neighborhoods are oozing with atmosphere.

NYC Lowlights

It's overwhelming – it's fast, expensive and crowded, and there's too much to see and do. It's too hot in summer and too cold in winter, and the shoulder seasons are too damn short. The hotel rooms are small, you've got to wait in line for the sights, elbow your way onto the subway and – sometimes – pay $10 for a sandwich.

Here's a subjective list of what we don't like; lots of people can handle this stuff, but it's not for us:

- pedestrian pasta and so-so scallopini in Little Italy
- door snobs at entertainment venues
- environmental unawareness (how many napkins do people need?)
- salad bars
- long brunch lines when you're really hungry

One lowlight: traffic jams

You may notice that you're not the only visitor in town, especially if you get stuck in a three-hour line for the Empire State Building. Avoid delays by getting up early in order to be among the first to arrive at every site. The **CityPass** (**e** www.citypass.net) lets you bypass ticket lines for five major attractions (and saves almost 50% on admission). Buy it at participating venues or pre-purchase via the website.

Stopping Over?

One Day Whiz up the Empire State Building to get your bearings, then take the subway to the Met for an art attack. Stroll back downtown through Central Park, perhaps hopping over to Madison Ave's boutiques. Take a taxi to Greenwich Village for dinner.

Two Days Catch the early ferry to the Statue of Liberty and Ellis Island. Afterward, take the subway to Midtown for a late lunch at the sunny cafés in Bryant Park and an edifying afternoon at the landmark public library.

Three Days After a lazy brunch over the *New York Times,* visit the American Museum of Natural History, then shop and gallery-hop in Soho till it's time to dine.

AMERICAN MUSEUM OF NATURAL HISTORY   (2, G4)

The museum was founded in 1869 on the basis of a mastodon's tooth and a few thousand beetles. Now there are more than 32 million artifacts in its collection. The most famous items take up the three large **dinosaur halls**, which present the latest theories about these behemoths' behavior and disappearance. Knowledgeable guides roam the halls ready to answer your questions, and 'please touch' displays let you get your hands all over the skullcap of a pachycephulosaurus, a herbivorous dinosaur that roamed the earth 65 million years ago.

The treasures of the four floors of the permanent collection include the scary-looking, life-size plaster blue whale hanging down from the ceiling above the **Hall of Ocean Life**. Newer exhibitions feature a strong ecological slant – the Hall of Biodiversity explores earth's diversity and the threat of environmental degradation.

While some of the mammal halls still suffer from a gloomy, Victorian-era look, the museum is aggressively updating the facility with 'electronic newspaper' video terminals and excellent look-and-learn displays.

Some state-of-the-art additions include an **IMAX** screen in a beautiful old theater and a spectacular **Center for Earth and Space**, with a planetarium and Big Bang Room, re-creating the birth of the universe. The Space Theater shows *Passport to the Universe*, narrated by a portentous Tom Hanks. It costs extra and can safely be missed.

INFORMATION

- ✉ Central Park W at W 79th St
- ☎ 769-5100
- 🚇 81st St
- 🚌 M79
- 🕐 10am-5:45pm (Fri-Sat to 8:45pm)
- 💲 suggested donation $10/6, $15/9 with IMAX, $19/11.50 with Space Show; temporary exhibits extra; CityPass good
- ℹ audio tours, free guided tours hourly 10:15am-3:15pm
- 🚼 Discovery Room
- ℮ www.amnh.org
- ♿ excellent
- 🍴 Museum Food Court, Cafe on 4, Cafe 77

Join the herd.

DON'T MISS
- Star of India • barosaurus • Cosmic Pathway • Hall of Meteorites
- giant sequoia tree • live jazz Friday evening in the Rose Center

BROOKLYN BRIDGE   (3, M8)

Regarded by many as the most beautiful bridge in the world and a magnificent example of fine urban design, the Brooklyn Bridge was the first steel suspension bridge ever built, and its 1568ft (478m) span between the two support towers was the world's longest when the bridge opened in 1883.

It remains a compelling symbol of US achievement and a superbly graceful structure, though its construction was plagued by budget overruns and the deaths of 20 workers, including designer John Roebling, the inventor of wire cable, who died of tetanus poisoning after being knocked off a pier in 1869. His son took over the project but then succumbed to the bends while working on the excavation and thereafter supervised operations from a telescope in his sick room. To top off the misfortune, 12 pedestrians were trampled during the opening ceremony, amid a panic that the bridge was collapsing.

There's no fear of collapse today, with the bridge well into its second century. The pedestrian walkway that begins just east of City Hall affords a wonderful view of Lower Manhattan, and you can stop at observation points under both stone support towers and view brass panorama histories of the waterfront at various points in New York's history.

Once you reach the Brooklyn side (about a 20-minute walk), you can bear right to walk down to Cadman Plaza West, leading to a park and to Middagh St, which passes through the heart of Brooklyn Heights. Continuing left brings you to Brooklyn's downtown area, which includes the ornate Borough Hall and Fulton St pedestrian mall.

Gateway to the city that never sleeps

Esbin-Anderson Photography

DON'T MISS

• a walk or bike ride across the bridge at sunset • an evening riverside promenade in Brooklyn Heights • boat trip under the bridge (p. 51-2)

CENTRAL PARK   (2, B5-K5)

This large rectangular park right in the middle of Manhattan helps to make New York liveable. On weekends, it's packed with joggers, skaters, musicians and tourists, but north of 72nd St the crowds thin out and it's easier to appreciate the landscaping. Though the park is quite safe during the day, it's best to stick to peopled areas after dark.

Central Park's 843 acres (337 hectares) were set aside in 1856, on the marshy northern fringe of the city. The project received wide support: the rich wanted a setting for pony and carriage rides while the socially minded wanted workers to have somewhere to unwind besides saloons. The naturalist landscaping was innovative, with forested groves, winding paths and informal ponds.

In the 1960s and '70s, the park hosted big rock concerts (Simon and Garfunkel appeared) and hippie 'be-ins.' The Public Theater, the Metropolitan Opera and the New York Philharmonic began **free summer performances** at the same time. Recent events have included shows by Erykah Badu and Chinese acrobats.

The roadway encircling the park and the path around the Jacqueline Kennedy Onassis Reservoir are ever popular with runners, in-line skaters and bikers. You can rent bikes and boats at the **Loeb Boathouse** (☎ 517-3623), on East Dr near 74th St. You can also ice-skate from October to May at the Wollman Rink (☎ 396-1010), at 62nd St, and at the less crowded Lasker Rink (same ☎), which is uptown near E 106th St.

INFORMATION

- ✉ bounded by 59th & 110th Sts, 5th Ave & Central Park W
- ☎ 794-6564 Dairy Visitor Center
- Ⓔ 5th Ave (N, R), Columbus Circle, 72nd St (B, C), 81st St, 86th St (B, C), 103rd St (B, C), Cathedral Pkwy (B, C), Central Park North
- 🚌 M1-5, M72, M79, M86
- ⏰ 6am-1am
- 🄴 www.centralpark.org
- ✕ Park View at the Boathouse (p. 82), Tavern on the Green (1 W 67th St; ☎ 873-3200), kiosks

Angus Oborn

Kim Grant

New York's year-round urban oasis

DON'T MISS
- The Ramble • Strawberry Fields • The Carousel • Wildlife Center
- urban fisherfolk at Harlem Meer • free Shakespeare in the Park

ELLIS ISLAND   (4, D2)

Ellis Island was New York's main immigration station from 1892 to 1954 – more than 12 million people passed through here. Its early years were busiest: in 1907 an all-time high of one million new Americans arrived. Later, Ellis Island also operated as a hospital for soldiers and a detention station for deportees and illegal aliens. When the island was abandoned in 1954, only one inmate needed to be rehoused: a sailor detained for the dastardly crime of overstaying his shore leave.

The impressive redbrick main building is now an **Immigration Museum**. The exhibitions begin at the Baggage Room and continue up to 2nd-story rooms where medical inspections took place. The doctors flew through their initial exams in six seconds; if further investigation was necessary, the immigrant's clothes were marked with chalk. Contrary to popular myth (or so the museum argues), most of the ship-borne immigrants were processed within eight hours, in conditions that were generally clean and safe.

'Telephones' connect you to the voices of Ellis Island immigrants, a film describes the immigrant experience, and exhibits show how the influx changed the USA. An interesting wall display features Tin Pan Alley sheet music that was aimed at the new foreign-born audience.

The Registry Room includes a beautiful vaulted tile ceiling made by immigrants from Spain. But walking though the registry today surely can't compare to the days when the same room housed a line of 5000 confused and tired people waiting to be interviewed by overworked immigration officers.

INFORMATION

- ✉ Ellis Island
- ☎ 363-3200, ferry info 269-5755
- 🚇 Bowling Green, South Ferry
- 🚌 M15
- ⛴ Circle Line ferry departs Battery Park every 20-30mins 8:30am-late afternoon, stops first at Liberty Island, then at Ellis Island; no ferry from Ellis Island to Liberty Island
- 🕐 museum 9am-5pm (June-Aug to 6:30pm)
- 💲 museum free, ferry $8/3-6
- ℹ audio tour $4/3
- 📧 www.nps.gov/elis
- ♿ excellent
- ✕ kiosk

Ellis Island: the first stop for millions

DON'T MISS
• exhibits: Through America's Gate, Ellis Island Chronicles and Treasures from Home • the play *Ellis Island Stories* • Immigrant Wall of Honor • views of Statue of Liberty and Manhattan

EMPIRE STATE BUILDING   (2, P6)

New York's original skyline symbol is a limestone classic built in just 410 days during the depths of the Depression for $41 million. The 102-story landmark opened in 1931 and immediately became the most exclusive business address in the city.

The famous antenna was originally intended to be a zeppelin mooring mast, but the Hindenberg disaster put a stop to that plan. One airship accidentally met up with the building: a B25 crashed into the 79th floor on a foggy day in July 1945, killing 14 people.

The tragic destruction of the World Trade Center's twin towers has made the Empire State building the tallest building in New York once again. About 16,000 people work here, and a staggering 35,000 people visit the observatories every day.

Reaching the observatories on the 86th and 102nd floors means standing in line for tickets and elevators on the concourse level and sometimes being confronted with another line at the top. To beat the

INFORMATION

- ⊠ 350 5th Ave at 34th St
- ☎ 736-3100
- Ⓗ Herald Sq, 33rd St
- ⊙ Mon-Fri 10am-midnight, Sat-Sun 9:30am-midnight (last elevators leave at 11:15pm)
- Ⓢ $9/4-7, children under 5 free; CityPass good
- ⓔ www.esbnyc.com
- ♿ good
- ✗ eateries on concourse

Wayne Walton

Dale Buckton

Unbeatable views from the Empire State

crowd, come early or late, or buy a combination ticket ($10-17), which includes the silly but fun **New York Skyride**, on the 2nd floor; the combo ticket line is always shorter, which gets you to the elevator faster.

Once you're at the top, stay as long as you want. Diagrams help to identify what you're gawking at with your plain old eyes or the coin-operated telescopes. You shouldn't have any trouble finding your hotel from up here.

Simon Bracken

Elevators? Pah!

Every February, there's a big foot race up the Empire State's 1860 stairs from the street level to the heights of the 102nd floor. The all-time record, held by Australian Paul Crake, is nine minutes, 37 seconds.

GREENWICH VILLAGE (3, G5)

One of the city's most popular neighborhoods, Greenwich Village stands for all things outlandish and bohemian. It began as a trading port for Indians, who liked the easy access to the shores of what is now Hoboken, New Jersey, just across the Hudson River. Dutch settlers established tobacco plantations, but their English successors gave the peaceful wooded area its name.

INFORMATION

- ✉ east to west from Broadway to Hudson St; north to south from 14th St to Houston St
- Ⓜ Christopher St, W 4th St
- ♿ narrow pavements
- ✕ see p. 74

Richard I'Anson

As city life gave rise to a large servant class, Greenwich Village became New York's most prominent black neighborhood until a lot of black residents sought better housing in Harlem just before the 1920s. The brownstone buildings they abandoned are now some of the most fashionable and valuable properties in the city.

The Village's reputation as a creative enclave can be traced back at least 100 years, when artists and writers like Walt Whitman, Edgar Allen Poe and Edna St Vincent Millay moved in. By the 1940s, the area had become a gathering place for gays.

New York University dominates the center of the Village and owns most of the property around **Washington Square Park**, a popular spot with students, street performers and drug dealers. Southwest of the park, a lively collection of cafés, shops and restaurants crowds the streets. Past 7th Ave is the West Village, a pleasant neighborhood of crooked streets loaded with important buildings – look for bronze landmark plaques explaining their significance. For a self-guided tour of Greenwich Village, see p. 48.

Washington Square Park: grooving to the beat in an offbeat 'hood

Richard I'Anson

DON'T MISS
- cafés • New York's narrowest house (p. 48) • Forbes Galleries • jazz clubs • Minetta Lane • baffling intersection of W 4th & W 11th Sts

GUGGENHEIM MUSEUM   (2, E6)

The inspired work of Frank Lloyd Wright, the sweeping spiral of the Guggenheim is a superb sculpture in and of itself; the excellent collection of 20th-century paintings housed inside is almost an afterthought. Solomon Guggenheim commissioned the landmark building in 1943, but construction did not commence until 1957. Wright died six months before his creation was finished in 1959. A controversial 1993 extension added a 10-story tower (by Gwathmey Siegel) that makes the museum look like a toilet, according to some.

The museum's permanent collection includes work by Picasso, Pollock, Chagall, Cézanne and (especially) Kandinsky. In 1976, Justin Thannhauser bequeathed his impressive collection of contemporary art, which now comprises the bulk of the museum's late-19th- and early-20th-century art, including pieces by Monet, Pissarro, van Gogh and Degas.

The museum's **collection of American minimalist art** from the 1960s and '70s got a boost from the acquired holdings of Panzo di Biumo in 1990. In 1993, the Robert Mapplethorpe Foundation donated 200 photographs, spurring the museum to devote the 4th floor of the tower to photography shows.

Temporary exhibitions, which are often drawn from private collections, take up the bulk of the spiral area; the museum's permanent collection generally hangs in the offshoot tower galleries. Though the exhibitions tend to work bottom to top, you could take the elevator to the 6th floor and let gravity help you make your way down. No matter which way you do it, though, you can't get lost – what a relief after wandering through the Met's maze.

INFORMATION

- ✉ 1071 5th Ave at 89th St
- ☎ 423-3500
- Ⓐ 86th St (4, 5, 6)
- 🚌 M1-4
- 🕐 Sun-Wed 9am-6pm, Fri-Sat 9am-8pm
- Ⓢ $12/8, children under 12 free; pay what you wish Fri evening; CityPass good
- ⓘ Fri & Sat evening jazz, regular films, daily tours, children & family programs
- Ⓔ www.guggenheim .org
- ♿ very good
- ✗ Museum Café

Greg Gawlowski

Rick Gerharter

The Guggenheim's dizzying spiral

- • Matisse's *The Italian Woman* • Kandinsky's *In the Black Square*
- • Mondrian's *New York City I* • van Gogh's *Peasants Lifting Potatoes*
- • Picasso's *Moulin de la Galette* • Cézanne's *Man with Crossed Arms*

METROPOLITAN MUSEUM OF ART   (2, G6)

Commonly called 'the Met,' this vast museum is New York's most popular single-site tourist attraction. When you enter the Great Hall, pick up a floor plan and work out what you'd most like to see before the Met's great riches wear you out. The first choice is between two ancient worlds: the Egyptian, to your right as you enter, and the Greek & Roman, to your left.

INFORMATION

- ✉ 5th Ave at 82nd St
- ☎ 535-7710
- Ⓗ 86th St (4, 5, 6)
- 🚍 M1-5
- 🕐 Tues-Thurs & Sun 9:30am-5:15pm, Fri-Sat 9:30am-8:45pm
- 💲 suggested donation $10/5, children under 12 free
- ⓘ audio tours $5, free guided tours
- e www.metmuseum .org
- ♿ good, wheelchairs available, tours for visually handicapped
- ✗ cafeteria, café, bar

The Metropolitan Museum of Art, © Bill Melton, Wild Bill Studios

Dale Buckton

Ancient Egypt lives on at the Met.

If you begin with the Egyptian art in the northern wing, start with the tomb of Pernebi, then keep left to pass several mummies and some incredibly well-preserved wall paintings. Farther on you come to the entire **Temple of Dendur**, which was saved from submersion in the waters behind the Aswan Dam.

Exit behind the temple and head to the **American Wing**, which starts with baseball cards. Continue left through exhibits of furniture and clocks. Along an enclosed garden are displays of Tiffany stained-glass and the entire facade of the Branch Bank of the US.

The dark **Medieval Galleries** are next, with artifacts, jewelry and religious art. Turn right to get to the Lehman Collection of Italian, impressionist and modern art. If you continue to the northeastern corner, you come upon the 20th-century art collection (and the elevator to the lovely roof garden).

Heading back toward 5th Ave, you will pass through the **Africa, Oceania & the Americas** rooms and into the new **Greek & Roman galleries**, before winding up back at the south side of the Great Hall. On the 2nd floor lie the Met's unrivaled collection of European paintings and the Asian art holdings.

DON'T MISS

- Sarcophagus of Har-khebi • de Kooning's *Woman* • Picasso's *The Dreamer* • van Gogh's *Cypresses* • works from Rodin's *The Gates of Hell* • music in the Great Hall Friday and Saturday evening

MUSEUM OF MODERN ART (2, M6)

Founded in 1929, the Museum of Modern Art (MoMA) has amassed a super collection that shouldn't be missed. From mid-2002 to early 2005, however, the bulk of the collection will be locked away while the 53rd St location is renovated and expanded. Meanwhile, you can view the greatest hits and some draw-card temporary shows in a converted Swingline staple factory in Queens. When the revamped museum opens, the temporary site will revert to a storage and research facility.

Don't be put off by the location – there's a subway right there – and with van Gogh's *Starry Night*, Picasso's *Les Demoiselles d'Avignon* and Matisse's *Dance I* on display, it would be worth going if you had to pogo there. Temporary exhibitions during the renovation period feature visionary architectural drawings, plus work by Matisse, Picasso, Max Beckmann, Ansel Adams and Kiki Smith, among others.

MoMA places a special emphasis on photography and film, with regular film screenings (free with your museum admission) from its archive of 20,000 film titles, plus a very impressive collection of film posters. An Oscar was awarded to the museum's film department in 1978. Screenings will continue at the temporary site.

While you're out in Queens, take advantage of shuttle buses linking MoMA with PS1 (p. 34) and other cultural offerings in the boroughs.

Angus Oborn

INFORMATION

- ✉ 11 W 53rd St btw 5th & 6th Aves; Queens: 45-20 33rd St at Queens Blvd, Long Island City (6, D2)
- ☎ 708-9480
- 5th Ave (E, F); Queens: 33rd St (7)
- M1-4
- 53rd St: Sat-Tues & Thurs 10:30am-6pm, Fri 10:30am-8:30pm; Queens: Thurs-Mon 10am-5pm (Fri to 7:45pm)
- $ $10/7, children under 16 free; pay what you wish Fri after 4:30pm; CityPass good
- e www.moma.org
- ♿ yes
- ✕ Sette MoMA Bar & Ristorante

Angus Oborn

Angus Oborn

Get an eyeful at MoMA.

Upside Down & Red-Faced

In 1961, Henri Matisse's *Le Bateau*, a gouache of a sailing boat and its reflection, hung upside down in MoMA for nearly two months before anyone noticed. The 116,000 visitors to the museum in this period included Matisse's son, Pierre.

NEW YORK PUBLIC LIBRARY   (2, O6)

Our favorite place in New York is a giant treasure chest of history, knowledge and atmosphere. Finished in 1911, the marble beaux arts building was constructed on the site of the old Croton Reservoir, which took two years to dismantle. Officially, it's the Humanities and Social Services Library (one of New York's four main libraries), but really this is *the* library.

INFORMATION

- ✉ 5th Ave at E 42nd St
- ☎ 930-0800
- Ⓜ 42nd St-Grand Central
- 🚌 M42
- 🕐 Mon & Thurs-Sat 10am-6pm, Tues & Wed 11am-7:30pm (hours changeable)
- $ free
- e www.nypl.org
- ♿ yes

Allan Montaine

Angus Oborn

The 15 million (and counting) objects on 75 miles (120km) of shelving include medieval manuscripts, comic books, Babylonian clay tablets, maps, Japanese scrolls, baseball cards and, of course, lots of books. Most fabulously, the general collections are freely available – anyone can walk in and call up a book. So, whether it's been bugging you that you can't remember where Wake Island is or you've got some research to do on Yiddish folk tales, you can enlighten yourself here. There's free Internet access, too – register early because it books up fast.

The special collections (not so freely available) house Thomas Jefferson's handwritten Declaration of Independence, the manuscript

Where the city's studious set gathers

of TS Eliot's *The Wasteland*, Shakespeare's first folio and novelist Charlotte Bronte's writing desk.

The heart of the building is the massive 3rd-floor **reading room**, with its cloud-painted ceilings and handsome long tables punctuated by original Tiffany lamps and Ethernet ports. Vladimir Nabokov penned a few words here, as did countless other novelists and academics. The library's exhibition spaces have featured topics like caricature, traveling theater troupes and the mapping of the west.

Lionizing

The famous lions guarding the steps of the library are known as Patience (to the south) and Fortitude (to the north). Sculpted from pink Tennessee marble by Edward Clark Potter, they've been adopted as the library's mascots.

NEW YORK STOCK EXCHANGE (3, N6)

Though 'Wall St' is the widely recognized metaphor for US capitalism, the world's best-known stock exchange is actually around the corner on Broad St, behind a portentous facade reminiscent of a Roman temple.

Free tickets allow entrance to the visitors' center in 45-minute time periods throughout the day and are usually snapped up by noon. While waiting in line, you'll see dozens of brokers, all wearing color-coordinated trading jackets, popping out of the NYSE for a quick cigarette or hot dog.

Once you get inside, don't waste too much time in the self-guided,

INFORMATION

✉ 8 Broad St at Wall St
☎ 656-5165
Ⓜ Wall St, Broad St
🚌 M6
🕐 call for open times
$ free (get tickets at 20 Broad St)
ⓔ www.nyse.com
♿ good
✗ Mangia (p. 78)

James Marshall

I'm in the Market for You

George Olsen's song reflects the Jazz Age optimism before the 1929 crash: 'I'll have to see my broker...cuz I'm in the market for you....You're going up, up, up in my estimation, I want a thousand shares of your caresses too....We'll count the hugs and kisses, when dividends are due, cuz I'm in the market for you.'

It's bear versus bull at the NYSE.

PR-oriented 'Interactive Education Center.' The modern business of the exchange isn't explained well, and the center makes no mention of the 1929 stock market crash or the 1987 debacle, which led to restrictions on the computer-programmed stock dumping that triggered it.

Keep going to the visitors' gallery overlooking the frenetic trading floor; attendants are on hand to explain what everyone is doing. Each of the NYSE's 1600 'seats' is worth about $2.6 million; the brokers here trade shares for 10,000 different companies.

At 4pm, a retiring broker or another worthy gets the honor of ringing a bell that brings the business day to a close. Cheers arise if the market closes on a high note; groans and oaths abound on a down day.

After the September 11 attacks, the NYSE suffered through its longest shutdown ever (one week) but soon reopened to take traders on a bumpy ride. At press time, it was closed to the public; call for updates.

ROCKEFELLER CENTER (2, M6)

Begun in 1931, the art deco Rockefeller Center took nine years to complete. Some 200 dwellings were removed to make way for the project, but at the time the residential destruction was less controversial than Mexican artist Diego Rivera's lobby mural, which depicted Lenin; it was covered during the opening ceremonies and later destroyed. Its replacement, painted by José Maria Sert, features the more acceptable Abraham Lincoln.

INFORMATION

✉ 48th St to 51st St btw 5th & 6th Aves

☎ 332-6868

🚇 Rockefeller Center

🚌 M1-7, M50

$ outdoor area and GE Bldg lobby free, skating $7.50-11/4-6 (skate rental $4-5)

ℹ Radio City Music Hall tour (☎ 632-4041) Mon-Sat 10am-5pm, Sun 11am-5pm ($15/9); NBC studio tour (☎ 664-3700) Mon-Sat 8:30am-5:30pm, Sun 9:30am-4:30pm ($17.50/15/21 combination with Rockefeller Center tour); Rockefeller Center tour (☎ 664-7174) departs from NBC Store 9:30am-4:30pm ($10/8).

e www.rockefeller center.com, www.radiocity.com, www.nbc.com

♿ good

✗ Rainbow by Cipriani (p. 97), Sea Grill (☎ 332-7610), Chez Louis (☎ 333-3388)

Kim Grant

Greg Gawlowski

Adorned with statuary and decorated facades, the center is at its best in winter, when the plaza becomes an **ice-skating rink** and the famous Christmas tree sparkles in the chill air. The ritual lighting of the tree, at the end of November, is a spectacle complete with skating shows, choirs and kids salivating over Santa.

Inside the center lies the recently restored **Radio City Music Hall**, a 6000-seat art deco palace – even the smoking rooms and toilets are elegant. Tickets to the annual Christmas pageant featuring the corny but enjoyable Rockettes cost $34-110.

The NBC television network maintains its New York headquarters in the GE Building. The **NBC Discovery Center**, in the base of the building, offers some free activities (you can be a weather reporter or a celebrity guest on *The Tonight Show with Jay Leno*). The expensive studio tour is fun but probably only worth it if you're a fan of the shows taped here *(Saturday Night Live, Late Night with Conan O'Brien* and *The Rosie O'Donnell Show). Today* is broadcast from 7am to 9am daily from the plaza south of the fountain area. See p. 100 for information about getting tickets to TV tapings.

DON'T MISS
• *Prometheus* statue • *Atlas* statue • frescoes on the GE Building
• Radio City tours • Rockefeller Center Plaza during the holidays

SOUTH STREET SEAPORT (3, M7)

The central New York port during the 'Golden Age of Sail' (mid-1800s), this seaport was the docking place for the famous *Flying Cloud* before she embarked on her record-breaking voyage to San Francisco via Cape Horn in 1851. It was also the main East River ferry dock but fell into disuse upon the building of the Brooklyn Bridge and the establishment of deepwater piers on the Hudson River.

Now restored, the 11-block enclave includes historic ships and buildings, an excellent series of small museums with a maritime bent and a lot of sterile shops and restaurants that draw tourist crowds. The **South Street Seaport Museum** oversees several interesting sights in the area, including two galleries, an antique printing shop, a memorial lighthouse to *Titanic* victims and a maritime crafts center. Several tall-masted sailing vessels, including the *Peking*, the *Wavertree*, the *Pioneer* and the lightship *Ambrose*, stand just south of Pier 17.

Pier 17 is also the site of the **Fulton Fish Market** (slated to relocate to the Bronx around 2003), where most of the city's restaurants get their fresh seafood from midnight to 8am. For great views of the East River bridges, head to the boring shopping center building behind the market.

Schermerhorn Row, a block full of old warehouses bordered by Fulton, Front and South Sts, contains a visitors' center, shops, restaurants and a pub. From Pier 16, you can take riverboat and schooner tours that highlight the city's maritime history.

Another new branch of the Guggenheim Museum is planned for the area spanning Piers 9, 11, 13 and 14, but it will take a number of years to build.

INFORMATION

- ✉ South St, visitors' center 12 Fulton St
- ☎ 748-8600
- Ⓢ Fulton St
- 🚌 M15
- ⏱ Apr-Sept 10am-6pm, Oct-Mar 10am-5pm (closed Tues)
- Ⓢ $5/free (includes admission to historic ships)
- ⓘ schooner tours (☎ 748-8786)
- ℮ www.southstseaport.com
- ♿ yes
- ✕ Paris Cafe (p. 78), Bridge Cafe (p. 78)

Catch of the day at Fulton Fish Market

Adina Tony Amsel

Kim Grant

STATUE OF LIBERTY   (4, D2)

This great statue, *Liberty Enlightening the World*, is an all-American icon. French sculptor Frédéric-Auguste Bartholdi spent 10 years in Paris making the 151ft (45m) figure, thought to be based on the face of his mother and the body of his mistress. The statue – which consists of a copper skin attached to an iron skeleton designed by Gustave Eiffel – was shipped to New York in 1886 and erected on a small island that used to house a gallows.

The official opening, held on October 28, 1886, was for dignitaries only, though a million people gathered for a celebratory parade down Broadway. Only two women were invited to the ceremonial lunch (held in the Lady's leg), provoking two miffed suffragettes to circle the island in a boat, shouting out megaphone protests during the proceedings.

Some 354 steps climb from the pedestal to the crown, and though the views from ground level are almost as good as those from the top, it's worth making the climb simply to be inside this colossal structure. In summer, only passengers on the first ferry get tickets to climb up to the crown; in autumn, the first two boatloads can go up. Later arrivals must stop at the base of the statue.

The ticket office for the Circle Line ferry is at Castle Clinton: the

INFORMATION

- ✉ Liberty Island
- ☎ 363-3200, ferry info 269-5755
- 🚇 Bowling Green, South Ferry
- 🚌 M15
- ⛴ Circle Line ferry departs Battery Park every 20-30mins 8:30am-late afternoon, stops first at Liberty Island, then continues to Ellis Island; no ferry from Ellis Island to Liberty Island
- 🕐 9am-5pm (June-Aug to 6:30pm)
- 💲 statue free, ferry $8/3-6
- 🄴 www.nps.gov/stli
- ♿ to base only
- ✗ kiosk

Lady Liberty's original torch

Kim Grant

Greg Gawlowski

She's a Big Girl

The Statue of Liberty has quite a honker – her nose is 53 inches (1.35m) long. Her ears – 3.3ft (1m) long – are so big that workers sat inside them during construction. The statue can sway about 4 inches (10cm) – if there's a breeze while you're up there, you'll feel it shifting.

boat stops first at Liberty Island, then Ellis Island before it makes its way back to Manhattan, with spectacular views all the way. Be sure to take a look at the flame, gilded in 24-carat gold leaf.

TIMES SQUARE   (2, N5)

Before TV, Times Square was *the* place for glittery advertising directed at a mass audience. Long celebrated as New York's crossroads, Times Square fell into a deep decline in the 1960s, as once-proud movie palaces turned into 'triple X' porn theatres, and the square became a hangout for every colorful, crazy or dangerous character in Midtown.

During the 1990s, the city finally sunk Times Square's gamy reputation, and today it's almost desperately family-friendly. These days you're more likely to see flashing logos than flashers, and corporations will chase after your bucks harder than the muggers ever did. Virgin Megastore, the neighboring Planet Hollywood and Walt Disney, among others, have taken over the new Times Square.

Strolling around here gives you a good look at the city's many architectural styles, from the art deco **McGraw Hill Building** (330 W 42nd St) to the Greek Revival **Town Hall** (113 W 43rd St) and the more modern and garish office blocks on Broadway itself, epitomized by the **Morgan Stanley Building** (1589 Broadway).

The neighborhood's oldest venue, the 1899 **New Victory Theater** (209 W 42nd St), hosts children's productions. The Disney Corporation has turned the **New Amsterdam** (214 W 42nd St), built in 1904, into a permanent home for its theatrical versions of classic children's tales. Madame Tussaud's Wax Museum (p. 41) and the BB King Blues Club & Grill (p. 90), a 550-seat nightclub and restaurant, have brought even more good, clean fun to the area.

INFORMATION

- ✉ junction 42nd St, 7th Ave & Broadway
- ☎ 768-1560
- 🚇 42nd St-Times Sq
- 🚌 M42, M104
- ① Times Square Visitors' Center (1560 Broadway btw 46th & 47th Sts), 8am-8pm: information, theater tickets, free Internet access, exchange facilities, free 2hr walking tour Fri noon
- ⓔ www.timessquarebid.org
- ♿ reasonable
- ✕ Planet Hollywood (Broadway at W 45th St; ☎ 840-8326)

The neon jungle: Times Square

DON'T MISS
• a drink in the Marriott Marquis revolving bar • New Year's Eve festivities • singing waitresses at Ellen's Stardust Diner (p. 94) • blockbuster Broadway musicals • walking tour from visitors' center

World Trade Center Site (3, M5)

For most of the last 25 years in New York, you always knew how to find north: you just put the World Trade Center behind you. Emerging from the subway, you took a reflex head-check for the gleaming twin towers (see photo at left) and then set on your way. But all of that changed on September 11, 2001. Now New Yorkers and their legions of visitors will spend the foreseeable future looking for a big hole in the skyline.

The World Trade Center twin towers took seven years to build, from 1966 to 1973. They stood 107 stories and 1330ft (405m) tall. Fittingly enough, when the biggest things in town fell, their collapse tore at the heart of the city, taking with them almost 4000 lives, the offices of hundreds of businesses, one of the finest viewpoints in all of Manhattan and the peace of mind of millions around the world.

It's a strange thing, visiting a place because it isn't there anymore. Only days after the terrorist attacks, the curious and the aggrieved alike started making their way to the long-smoking rubble at 'Ground Zero,' honing in on the choking stench as the restricted zone shrunk. Motives differ for having a look: it's paying tribute and rubber-necking all at once – no matter what your reasons, though, you'll probably end up feeling shattered. Be sensitive – most residents take offense at tourists snapping photos.

Two months after the attacks, walls of remembrance and impromptu memorials (see photo at right) still dotted the downtown area, as New York came to grips with the magnitude of its loss. But despite the devastation, the city was discovering a new sense of community, offering some unusual sights to visitors: strangers chatting on the subway, hardened cops comforting the afflicted and New Yorkers of all stripes standing on the streets, wiping away tears.

The indelibly altered skyline of Lower Manhattan

sights & activities

MANHATTAN NEIGHBORHOODS

Sometimes called the 'city of neighborhoods,' New York features plenty of colorful pockets. While you're in town, check out some of these 'hoods, listed roughly from south to north.

Lower Manhattan, the southern tip of the island, includes historical sites from the Dutch period and earlier, as well as the fabled **Financial District**, home of Wall St and the tragic site of the terrorist attacks on September 11, 2001. To the north, Manhattan's famous **Chinatown** runs roughly east to west from the Bowery to Broadway and north to south from Grand St to Chatham Square.

Old warehouses and funky restaurants dot **Tribeca** (which comes from the phrase 'Triangle below Canal St'), roughly bordered by Broadway and Chambers St. Fashion photographers come here for the desolation chic.

Centered on Mulberry St north of Canal St, **Little Italy** has become a bit of a tourist trap. North of Broome St, the area segues into **Nolita** ('North of Little Italy'), a cool fashion and food district. Nearby, the **Lower East Side**, longtime enclave of Jewish New Yorkers, is turning into two distinct areas on either side of Delancey St: to the south, it's drawing Chinese immigrants; to the north, it's becoming a yuppified adjunct of the East Village.

The cast-iron industrial buildings in **Soho** ('South of Houston St') once housed textile factories but were colonized by artists in the 1950s. Today, Soho, which extends down to Canal St, is full of galleries and boutiques.

North of Soho and Houston St lies the famous bohemian gathering place, **Greenwich Village** (p. 18), which runs from Broadway to Hudson St. The **West Village**, which helped give birth to the US gay rights movement in the 1960s, still boasts an active gay and lesbian community. The hip **East Village** – bordered by 14th St, Lafayette St, E Houston St and the East River – includes **Alphabet City** (Aves A, B, C and D), a dangerous and druggy area until recently; it's now scrubbed fairly clean.

Richard I'Anson

City sidewalks, busy sidewalks

Chelsea, west of Broadway between 14th and 23rd Sts, once contained dry-goods and retail stores, but today it brims with cafés, art galleries and gay and straight nightlife. To the east, the overlapping neighborhoods of the **Flatiron District** and **Gramercy Park** (with four historic parks – Union Square, Gramercy, Madison Square and Stuyvesant) are happening places to hang out, shop and eat.

Teeming **Midtown** (34th St to 59th St) holds many of the city's most popular attractions. The area includes **Rockefeller Center** (p. 24), **Times Square** (p. 27), the theater district and Grand Central Terminal. To the west is **Hell's Kitchen**, a gentrifying area of bars and remnant sleaze that some clean-living folks are trying to rename **Clinton**.

East of Midtown lies New York's most planned neighborhood, **Roosevelt Island**, a slim cut of land no wider than a football field in the East River. An aerial tramway scoots over from Manhattan in three minutes.

Home to New York's greatest concentration of cultural centers, the **Upper East Side** features Museum Mile, on 5th Ave above 57th St, as well as exclusive hotels and residences. Some stunning brownstone buildings line the side streets. On the other side of Central Park, the **Upper West Side** provides comfortable living for moneyed families. Many celebrities reside in the plush apartment buildings that line Central Park W up to 96th St.

North of Central Park, the city's most identifiable African American neighborhood, **Harlem**, includes gospel churches, jazz clubs and the Apollo Theater. Though there are racial tensions here, a conspicuous police presence keeps most danger at bay. **Spanish Harlem** (El Barrio) is home to a big Latino community. La Marqueta (Park Ave above 110th St) – a colorful collection of fruit and vegetable stalls – is the signature attraction.

Washington Heights is an unremarkable series of large apartment buildings at the northern tip of Manhattan, above Harlem. But the area around the Cloisters, which includes Fort Tryon Park, can make a beautiful escape in warm weather.

Brooklyn Hangouts

New York's most populous borough has lots to offer. **Williamsburg** is a postmodernist-meets-Polish blend of hipsters, pierogies and religious Jews. **Brooklyn Heights** features Lower Manhattan views, handsome brownstones and good restaurants. In **Park Slope**, young professionals and lesbians have added variety to established Hispanic communities. Along with ritzier **Cobble Hill**, it's an up-and-coming nightlife area. Farther afield is **Brighton Beach**, an enclave for Russian immigrants, and **Coney Island**, a fab destination for an afternoon out (p. 50).

A different Barney's: the Brooklyn version

Angus Oborn

MUSEUMS

Many small countries would burst with cultural pride if they had half of New York City's museums. From major art galleries to small community-based venues and oft-neglected outer-borough institutions, the museums in New York make this one of the richest art and culture zones in the world.

American Craft Museum (2, M5)

This three-story museum gets crafty with beading, origami, jewelry and relatively modest endeavors such as table settings and the art of the sandwich. All exhibitions are temporary – a recent show featured the stained-glass work of architect Frank Lloyd Wright.
✉ 40 W 53rd Street btw 5th & 6th Aves ☎ 956-3535 e www.american craftmuseum.org ⊕ 5th Ave (E, F), Queens: 33rd St (7) ▣ M1-4 ⏲ Tues-Sun 10am-6pm (Thurs to 8pm) ⑤ $7.50/4, children under 12 free; pay what you wish Thurs 6-8pm ♿ yes

Brooklyn Museum of Art (6, G2)

New York's second-biggest art museum has excellent collections of African, Islamic and Asian art, Egyptian mummy casings and classical antiquities. The permanent collection also includes 58 works by Auguste Rodin. Diverse and sometimes controversial temporary exhibitions have ranged from ancient Iranian ceramics to digital printmaking.
✉ 200 Eastern Pkwy, Brooklyn ☎ 718-638-5000 e www.brooklyn art.org ⊕ Eastern Pkwy-Brooklyn Museum ▣ B41, B48, B71 ⏲ Wed-Sun 10am-5pm ⑤ $6/3, children 12 & under free ♿ yes

The Cloisters (4, A2)

This lovely complex incorporates fragments of old French and Spanish monasteries. Since 1938, it's housed the Met's collection of medieval frescoes, tapestries and paintings, most of them donated by John D Rockefeller Jr.
✉ Fort Tryon Park, Washington Heights ☎ 923-3700 e www .metmuseum.org ⊕ 190th St ▣ M4 ⏲ Tues-Sun 9:30am-4:45pm (to 5:15pm Mar-Oct) ⑤ $5-10, children under 12 free; free with Metropolitan Museum of Art ticket

Dia Center for the Arts (3, D2)

This nonprofit organization has been hosting long-term exhibitions of contemporary art for two decades. Five floors of capital-A art begin with the lobby tiled by Jorge Pardo. Off-site installations include the Earth Room (141 Wooster St) and the Broken Kilometer (393 W Broadway).
✉ 548 W 22nd St btw 10th & 11th Aves ☎ 989-5566 e www .diacenter.org ⊕ 23rd St (C, E) ▣ M23 ⏲ Wed-Sun noon-6pm ⑤ $6/3, children under 10 free ♿ partial

El Museo del Barrio (2, B6)

The permanent collection of Puerto Rican, Caribbean and Latin American art includes pre-Columbian carved wooden saints, Mexican masks and Haitian voodoo flags. The museum's temporary

A contemplative moment at the Cloisters

exhibits keep up a dialogue between resident Latino communities and their countries of origin.
✉ 1230 5th Ave at 104th St ☎ 831-7272 e www.elmuseo.org ⊕ 103rd St (6) ▣ M1-4 ⏲ Wed-Sun 11am-5pm ⑤ $5/2 ♿ yes

The Frick's grand interior

Frick Collection (2, J6)

An outstanding private collection of European paintings features works by Bellini, Rembrandt, Titian, Vermeer, Reynolds and Constable. The 1914 mansion was part of the 5th Ave 'millionaires' row' of robber baron homes.

✉ 1 E 70th St at 5th Ave ☎ 288-0700
e www.frick.org
🚇 68th St (4, 5, 6)
🚌 M1-4 ⊙ Tues-Sat 10am-6pm, Sun 1-6pm
⑤ $10/5 (no children under 10) ♿ yes

International Center of Photography

(2, N5) The city's most important photography showplace has moved to smart new Midtown digs and expanded its offerings to incorporate photography-based video and sculpture installations. The artist retrospectives and theme exhibitions are usually excellent.

✉ 1133 6th Ave at

Museum Mile

On the second Tuesday in June, upper 5th Ave closes to traffic, and all area museums are free.

43rd St ☎ 860-1777
e www.icp.org
🚇 42nd St-Times Sq
⊙ Tues-Thurs 10am-5pm, Fri 10am-8pm, Sat-Sun 10am-6pm
⑤ $8/6, children under 12 free; pay what you wish Fri 5-8pm ♿ yes

Intrepid Sea, Air & Space Museum (2, N2)

This somewhat scrappy exhibit will please war machinery fans and spook pacifists. But even draft-dodging eyes might be impressed by the Intrepid aircraft carrier and the world's fastest plane (the A12 Blackbird). You can see the Berlin Wall fragment without paying admission.

✉ Pier 86, W 46th St at 12th Ave ☎ 245-0072 e www.intrepid museum.org 🚇 42nd St-Port Authority, 50th St (C, E) 🚌 M50
⊙ Apr-Sept Mon-Fri 10am-5pm, Sat-Sun 10am-7pm; Oct-Mar Tues-Sun 10am-5pm
⑤ $12/2-9; CityPass good ♿ partial

Isamu Noguchi Garden Museum

(6, C1) More than 250 examples of the Japanese-American sculptor's work are beautifully presented in 13 galleries and a tranquil garden that he designed himself.

✉ 32 Vernon Blvd at 33rd Rd, Long Island City, Queens ☎ 718-721-1932 e www.noguchi.org 🚇 Broadway (15min walk)
🚌 call for shuttle bus info ⊙ Apr-Oct Wed-Fri 10am-5pm, Sat-Sun 11am-6pm; free guided tour 2pm ⑤ $4/2
♿ partial

Jacques Marchais Center of Tibetan Art

(1 mile south of 4, E2) The Buddha statues, clothing and religious objects in the Tibetan-temple-style building make up one of the largest private collections of Tibetan art outside China.

✉ 338 Lighthouse Ave, Staten Island ☎ 718-987-3500 e www.tibetanmuseum.com
🚇 Staten Island Railway to Grant City
🚌 S74 to Lighthouse Ave (then 15min walk uphill) 🚢 Staten Island
⊙ Apr-Nov Wed-Sun 1-5pm, Dec-Mar Wed-Fri 1-5pm; call ahead for special Sun events
⑤ $5/2-3 (more for Sun events)

The restful grounds of the Jacques Marchais Center

Jewish Museum

(2, E6) Artifacts, dioramas and videos explore Jewish life past and present. The changing exhibits focus on prominent Jews (eg, Russian artist Marc Chagall), Jewish communities (eg, Morocco) and art. A large theater shows films and TV shows.

✉ 1109 5th Ave at 92nd St ☎ 423-3200

e www.thejewish
museum.org 🚇 96th St
(6) 🚌 M1-4 🕐 Sun-
Thurs 11am-5:45pm
(Tues to 8pm) ⑤ $8/5,
children under 12 free;
pay what you wish Tues
5:45-8pm ♿ yes

Lower East Side Tenement Museum (3, J8)
Get a handle on life for the
Lower East Side's immi-
grants by joining an evoca-
tive tour through tenement
apartments. The Confino
Family Apartment tour is
great if you're with kids.
✉ 90 Orchard St at
Broome St ☎ 431-0233
e www.tenement.org
🚇 Delancey St, Essex
St, Grand St 🚌 M15
🕐 visitors' center
11am-5pm; tours Tues-
Fri 1-4pm, Sat-Sun
11am-4:30pm (reserva-
tions advised) ⑤ $9/7

Museum for African Art (3, H6)
This vibrant collection
includes sculpture, cos-
tumes, masks and architectural designs focusing on
sub-Saharan Africa.
Storytelling, dance per-
formances and workshops
re-create African life.
✉ 593 Broadway btw
Houston & Prince Sts
☎ 966-1313 **e** www
.africanart.org
🚇 Broadway-Lafayette
St, Prince St 🚌 M21
🕐 Tues-Fri 10:30am-
5:30pm, Sat-Sun noon-
6pm ⑤ $5/2.50 ♿ yes

Museum of American Folk Art (2, M5)
Portraits, needlework,
scrimshaw and an iconic
Statue of Liberty weather-
vane are highlights of this
important collection of
work by self-taught artists.

Upper East Side stop
Kim Grant

The new building, which
opened in late 2001,
reflects the hands-on
nature of its contents; it
was partly made by hand.
✉ 45 W 53rd St btw
5th & 6th Aves ☎ 977-
7170 **e** www.folkart
museum.org 🚇 53rd St
(E, F) 🚌 M1-7 🕐 Tues-
Sun 10am-6pm (Fri to
8pm) ⑤ $9/5 ♿ yes

Museum of Chinese in the Americas (3, K6)
A recent installation in this
museum, which focuses on
Chinese American history,
communities and identity,
allowed visitors to take a
trip through 10 different
American Chinatowns. The
permanent collection in-
cludes wonderful Canton-
ese opera costumes.
✉ 2nd fl, 70 Mulberry
St at Bayard St ☎ 619-
4785 **e** www.moca-
nyc.org 🚇 Canal St (N,
R, S) 🕐 Tues-Sat noon-
5pm ⑤ $3/1, children
under 12 free

Museum of Television & Radio (2, M6)
This is a couch potato's
paradise, with more than
100,000 TV and radio
shows on the menu. Along
with scheduled programs
(maybe Miles Davis, maybe
Mr Bean), admission buys

you 2hrs viewing or listening in a private booth – go
early to secure a spot.
✉ 25 W 52nd St btw
5th & 6th Aves ☎ 621-
6800 **e** www.mtr.org
🚇 5th Ave (E, F)
🚌 M1-7 🕐 Tues-Sun
noon-6pm (Thurs to
8pm, Fri to 9pm)
⑤ $6/3-4 ♿ yes

New Museum of Contemporary Art
(3, H6) This place stays at
the vanguard of the con-
temporary scene by show-
ing installations, video,
painting and sculpture with
a global outlook. Down-
stairs, check out the great
art bookshop and the
Media Z lounge.
✉ 583 Broadway btw
Houston & Prince Sts
☎ 219-1222 **e** www
.newmuseum.org
🚇 Broadway-Lafayette
St, Prince St 🚌 M21
🕐 Tues-Sun noon-6pm
(Thurs to 8pm) ⑤ $6/3,
children under 18 free;
free Thurs 6-8pm ♿ yes

New-York Historical Society Museum
(2, H4) New York City's
oldest museum boasts a
quirky permanent collec-
tion, including the holdings
of Luman Reed, an early
patron of American art.
Changing exhibits focus on
locals, making this a great
place to get insight into
the New York psyche. The
Kid City exhibit offers a
child-size bite of the Big
Apple.
✉ 2 W 77th St at
Central Park W
☎ 873-2400 **e** www
.nyhistory.org 🚇 81st
St 🚌 M10, M79
🕐 Tues-Sat 11am-5pm
⑤ $5/3, children under
12 free ♿ yes

PS1 (6, D1)
Queens' cultural epicenter is this MoMA-run contemporary art center in an old school building. Installations, animation, sound art and interactive electronic media are just some of the noncanvas works by PS1's roster of emerging artists. Exhibitions take place indoors and out. Call for a schedule of special events. ✉ **22-25 Jackson Ave at 46th Ave, Long Island City, Queens** ☎ **718-784-2084** e **www.ps1 .org** 🚇 **23rd St-Ely Ave, 45th Rd-Courthouse Sq** 🚌 **Q67, B61** ⏰ **Wed-Sun noon-6pm** 💲 **$4/2** ♿ **yes**

Studio Museum in Harlem (1, C5)
A leading showcase of African American art with a well-respected artist-in-residence program, this museum includes the work of photographer James Van Der Zee, who chronicled the Harlem Renaissance of the 1920s and '30s, and objects from the Caribbean and Africa. ✉ **144 W 125th St at Powell Blvd** ☎ **864-4500** e **www.studio museum.org** 🚇 **125th St (2, 3)** 🚌 **M101** ⏰ **Wed-Thurs 10am-5pm, Fri 10am-8pm, Sat-Sun 10am-6pm** 💲 **$5/1-3** ♿ **yes**

Whitney Museum of American Art (2, H6)
The Whitney specializes in contemporary American art, with works by Hopper, Pollock, Rothko, de Kooning, O'Keeffe and Johns. Its biennial exhibition of artists-of-the-moment never fails to stir up controversy, and its digital art shows keep one foot in the future. ✉ **945 Madison Ave at E 75th St** ☎ **570-3676** e **www.whitney.org** 🚇 **77th St** 🚌 **M1-4** ⏰ **Tues-Thurs & Sat-Sun 11am-6pm, Fri 1-9pm** 💲 **$10/8; pay what you wish Fri 6-9pm** ♿ **yes**

ART GALLERIES

New York City's more than 500 galleries tend to cluster in Soho, Chelsea or along 57th St. In recent years, some have spilled over into Williamsburg, Brooklyn. The monthly *Gallery Guide* is available free in most galleries; the Sunday *New York Times* is also a good place to look for gallery schedules.

Deitch Projects (3, J5)
This gallery sponsors innovative art onsite or on the streets. Previously exhibited artists include Jeff Koons, Japanese video artist Mariko Mori and Oleg Kulik, a Russian whose 'exhibition' was acting like a dog for two weeks. ✉ **76 Grand St btw Wooster & Greene Sts** ☎ **343-7300** 🚇 **Canal St (A, C, E)** ⏰ **Tues-Sat noon-6pm** ♿ **yes**

Exit Art (3, H6)
This big upstairs space with a nonthreatening co-op vibe features exhibits by emerging artists and off-beat retrospectives on subjects such as LP cover art. Performances take place in the intimate theater. ✉ **548 Broadway btw Prince & Spring Sts** ☎ **966-7745** 🚇 **Prince St, Spring St (6)** ⏰ **Tues-Fri 10am-6pm, Sat 11am-6pm** 💲 **$2**

Gagosian Gallery (3, C2; 2, H6) This big-name gallery represents Anselm Kiefer, Chris Burden and Philip Taafe. Gagosian's enthusiasm for Damien Hirst helped introduce the Yorkshireman to a skeptical US audience. The downtown venue is the place for theatrics and spectacle; uptown is more traditional. ✉ **downtown: 555 W 24th St at 11th Ave, uptown: 980 Madison Ave at 76th St** ☎ **downtown: 741-1111, uptown: 744-2313** e **www.gagosian .com** 🚇 **uptown: 77th St** 🚌 **downtown: M1-4, uptown: M23** ⏰ **Tues-Sat 10am-6pm** 💲 **free** ♿ **yes**

Galleries galore in Soho

Angus Oborn

Joseph Helman Gallery (2, L6)

Arresting contemporary American and European paintings, sculptures and installations are featured in this lovely large space.

✉ 20 W 57th St btw 5th & 6th Aves ☎ 245-2888 🚇 57th St (B, Q) 🚌 M57 ⏰ Tues-Sat 10am-6pm ⑤ free ♿ yes

Leo Castelli (2, G7)

This Italian art dealer 'discovered' many major artists, including Jasper Johns, Robert Rauschenberg and Roy Liechtenstein. Castelli moved his original 77th St premises to Soho in 1971, helping to begin the downtown art boom, but then led the Soho exodus and headed back north. Castelli died in 1999, but his artistic legacy survives.

✉ 59 E 79th St btw Park & Madison Aves ☎ 249-4470 🖥 www .castelligallery.com 🚇 77th St 🚌 M1-4 ⏰ Mon-Fri 11am-5pm ⑤ free

Mary Boone Gallery

(3, C2; 2, L6) Once jailed for handing out live ammunition to gallery goers, Boone continues to shake things up by showing the work of Ross Bleckner, Brice Marden, Julian Schnabel and others in her skylit Chelsea gallery. Her 5th Ave location draws an uptown crowd.

✉ downtown: 541 W 24th St btw 10th & 11th Aves, uptown: 745 5th Ave at 57th St ☎ 752-2929 🚇 downtown: 23rd St (C, E), uptown: 57th St (B, Q) ⏰ Tues-Sat 10am-6pm ⑤ free ♿ yes

Edwin-Anderson Photography

Subway Art

It's not just 'writers' (graffiti artists) who make a mark in the subways – professional artists' work can also be seen at many stations. Our favorites include Tom Otterness' sculptures in the 14th St (A, C, E) station; Faith Ringold, Maya Link and Mary Miss at Union Square; and modern mosaics at Lexington-59th St and the Lincoln Center stop. Big names at Times Square include Roy Lichtenstein.

Matthew Marks

(3, C2; 3, D2) This top-notch gallery features a stellar cast spread over two Chelsea locations. Artists exhibited include Willem de Kooning, Nan Goldin, Tracey Moffat, Jean-Marc Bustamante, Lucian Freud, Ellsworth Kelly and Andreas Gursky.

✉ 523 W 24th St at 10th Ave, 522 W 22nd St at 10th Ave ☎ 243-0200, 243-1650 🚇 23rd St (C, E) ⏰ 24th St: Mon-Fri 10am-6pm, 22nd St: Mon-Fri 11am-6pm ⑤ free ♿ yes

Paula Cooper (3, D2)

A longtime New York heavyweight, Cooper displays contemporary art in all media, including music installations. Consistently interesting shows have included work by Jonathan Borofsky, Dan Flavin, Zoe Leonard, Sherrie Levine and Andres Serrano.

✉ 534 W 21st St btw 10th & 11th Aves ☎ 255-1105 🚇 23rd St (C, E) 🚌 M23 ⏰ Tues-Sat 10am-6pm ⑤ free ♿ yes

Tony Shafrazi Gallery

(3, H5) An extremely versatile gallery with a populist outlook, this spot has shown work by David LaChapelle, Keith Haring, Andy Warhol, Michael Ray Charles and Dennis Hopper (when he's wearing his photography hat). It also manages the estate of Francis Bacon.

✉ 119 Wooster St btw Prince & Spring Sts ☎ 274-9300 🚇 Spring St (C, E), Prince St ⏰ Tues-Sat 10am-6pm ⑤ free ♿ yes

Williamsburg Art & Historical Center

(6, E2) For five years now, the WAH Center has been giving Brooklyn artists an airing in this shabbily handsome building. The gallery was founded by Yuko Nii, a Japanese-American artist, who has worked hard to create a Brooklyn artistic 'salon.'

✉ 135 Broadway at Bedford Ave, Brooklyn ☎ 718-486-7372 🖥 www.wahcenter.org 🚇 Bedford Ave, Marcy Ave ⏰ Sat-Sun noon-6pm ⑤ free

NOTABLE BUILDINGS

Many significant structures dot the area from Lower Manhattan to Midtown, and the Wall St environs offer an unrivaled museum of architecture, with Federal homes, Gothic churches, Renaissance palazzos and the world's finest collection of skyscrapers from the early 20th century.

Kim Grant
Chrysler's distinctive spire

Chrysler Building
(2, N7) Motorcar motifs adorn William van Alen's 1930 art deco masterpiece. Sadly, visitors are restricted to admiring the interior and the African marble onyx lights in the lobby. The building's needle-sharp stainless-steel spire is illuminated at night.
✉ 405 Lexington Ave at 42nd St Ⓜ 42nd St-Grand Central 🚌 M42, M101-104 ⌚ Mon-Fri 7am-6pm

Customs House (3, O5)
This is simply one of the most sumptuous beaux arts buildings ever built. Marine murals festoon the interior. An uncredited sketch of Greta Garbo, at a dockside press conference, is in the rotunda (toward the right rear). The engrossing Museum of the American Indian, inside the Customs House, belongs to the Smithsonian Institution.
✉ 1 Bowling Green ☎ 668-6624 Ⓜ Bowling Green 🚌 M6, M15 ⌚ 10am-5pm (Thurs to 8pm) $ free ♿ yes

City Hall (3, L6)
Among the first ostentatious buildings constructed in the city, this French Renaissance marble monster – now a working landmark – has been home to the city's government since 1812.
✉ Park Row ☎ 788-6865 Ⓜ City Hall ⌚ call to arrange tours $ free ♿ yes

Equitable Building
(3, N5) The sheer unapologetic bulk of this 41-story building, which opened just before WWI, changed the shape of Manhattan – and world architecture – forever. Its size created such an uproar that four years after it was built, New York enacted the nation's first zoning laws requiring building setbacks.
✉ 120 Broadway btw Pine & Cedar Sts Ⓜ Wall St 🚌 M6 ⌚ Mon-Fri 7am-7pm $ free ♿ yes

Federal Hall (3, N6)
The finest surviving example of classical architecture in Lower Manhattan, this 1842 building stands on the site of the old City Hall, where Washington took his oath of office in 1789 and where the city's courts, libraries, fire trucks and jail cells used to be. Check out the historical exhibitions inside.
✉ 26 Wall St at Broad St ☎ 825-6888 e www.nps.gov/feha Ⓜ Wall St, Broad St 🚌 M6 ⌚ 9am-5pm; guided tours 12:30-3:30pm $ free ♿ yes

The world's first skyscraper

Flatiron Building
(3, D5) Back in 1902, people were terrified that all 22 stories of the world's first skyscraper would topple. Still standing, it's been famously featured in a haunting 1905 Edward Steichen photo, and it remains a popular photo subject.
✉ intersection of Broadway, 5th Ave & 23rd St Ⓜ 23rd St (N, R) 🚌 M2, M3, M5-7, M23

General US Grant National Memorial

(1, C2) Civil War hero and former US president Ulysses S Grant and his wife, Julia, are buried at this landmark monument; it's the largest mausoleum in the country.

✉ **Riverside Dr at W 122nd St** ☎ 666-1640 **e** www.nps.gov/gegr ⊕ 116th St-Columbia University (1, 9) 🚌 M4, M104 ⊙ 9am-5pm ⑤ free

Grand Central Terminal (2, N7)

The interior of this beaux arts train terminal is breathtaking, especially its ceiling star map (notice that the pattern was mistakenly laid out backwards, as if the stars are being seen from above). Vanderbilt Hall hosts art exhibitions, and a constant parade of commuters provides plenty of theater. The Campbell Apartment (p. 97) and Oyster Bar (☎ 490-6650) make for excellent interludes.

✉ **Park Ave at 42nd St** ☎ 340-2210 **e** www.grandcentralterminal.com ⊕ 42nd St-Grand Central 🚌 M42 ⊙ 5:30am-1:30am ⑤ free ♿ yes

Puck Building (3, H6)

Home to the turn-of-the-century humor magazine, this stunning redbrick building features two gold-leaf statues of the portly Puck. It's a popular spot for wedding receptions and film shoots (you might recognize it from the TV show *Will & Grace*).

✉ **295 Lafayette St at Houston St** ⊕ Broadway-Lafayette St

Shrine of St Elizabeth Ann Seton (3, O6)

Dedicated to the first American Catholic saint, this shrine includes a church and an adjoining delicate Georgian home – the lone survivor of a series of graceful row houses that once hugged the shoreline.

✉ **7 State St at Pearl St** ☎ 269-6865 ⊕ South Ferry, Bowling Green, Whitehall St ⊙ church Mon-Fri 6:30am-5:30pm, Sun masses 9am & noon ⑤ free

United Nations (2, N8)

Designed by a committee of architects from around the world, the UN headquarters are very much international territory. Lobby exhibitions are free. While you're here, take a stroll through the nearby gardens and sculpture park, which feature some prime river views

✉ **1st Ave at 46th St** ☎ 963-7713 **e** www.un.org/Overview/Tours/UNHQ ⊕ 42nd St-Grand Central 🚌 M15, M27, M50, M104 ⊙ 9:30am-4:45pm (Jan-Feb closed Sat-Sun); tours every 30mins ⑤ $7.50/4-6 (no children under 5) ♿ yes

Woolworth Building

(3, M5) This was the world's tallest building when it was completed in 1913. Discount-store magnate Frank Woolworth reputedly paid the $15 million for this 'Cathedral of Commerce' with nickels and dimes. Crane your neck to view the extraordinary ceiling mosaic.

✉ **233 Broadway btw Park Pl & Barclay St** ⊕ City Hall 🚌 M6 ⊙ lobby open 24hrs ♿ yes

---

Sweet Nothings

There's a whispering gallery at **Grand Central Terminal** (p. 37) where three halls converge under a vaulted ceiling, outside the Oyster Bar on the lower level. Two people can communicate by standing in diagonal corners, facing away and whispering into the corner. The main hall at **Ellis Island** (p. 16) also conducts whispers – stand facing out over the balcony and test it out.

The hectic halls of Grand Central

Angus Oborn

PLACES OF WORSHIP

Cathedral of St John the Divine (2, A3)

This Episcopal cathedral is the USA's largest place of worship and the world's biggest Gothic cathedral. Construction began in 1892 and is continuing – look up to see sculptors carving in the stone! It hosts concerts, lectures and memorial services for famous New Yorkers. High Mass (Sun 11am) often features sermons by well-known intellectuals.

✉ 1047 Amsterdam Ave at 112th St ☎ 316-7540 ℮ www .stjohndivine.org Ⓔ Cathedral Parkway, 116th St-Columbia University (1, 9) 🚌 M4, M11 ⊘ 7:30am-6pm; tours Tues-Sat 11am, Sun 1pm ($3) Ⓢ $2 donation ♿ partial, via the 113th St entrance

Eldridge St Synagogue (3, J7)

This landmark Moorish synagogue is across the street from the city's oldest surviving blocks of tenements.

✉ 12 Eldridge St btw Division & Canal Sts ☎ 219-0888 Ⓔ E Broadway 🚌 M15 ⊘ tours Sun 11am-4pm,

St Patrick's: New York's grand Gothic cathedral

Tues & Thurs 11:30am & 2:30pm Ⓢ $4/2.50 ♿ yes

Riverside Church (1, D2)

This 1930 Gothic marvel, built by the Rockefellers, features an observation deck, the world's largest set of carillon bells and a theater and events program.

✉ 490 Riverside Dr at 120th St ☎ 870-6700 ℮ www.theriverside churchny.org Ⓔ 125th St (1, 9) 🚌 M5 ⊘ 7am-10pm Ⓢ free ♿ yes

St Patrick's Cathedral (2, M6)

Built in the French Gothic style, one of the city's greatest cathedrals serves the 2.2 million Catholics in the NY diocese (but can seat a mere 2400 of them).

✉ 50th St at 5th Ave ☎ 753-2261 Ⓔ 5th Ave (E, F), Rockefeller Center 🚌 M50 ⊘ 6am-9pm; guided tours ♿ yes

St Paul's Chapel (3, M6)

Designed in 1764, the area's last colonial building features fluted Corinthian columns and Waterford chandeliers. President Washington attended services in the airy interior of this Georgian chapel; his personal pew is still on display.

✉ Broadway at Fulton St ☎ 602-0800 Ⓔ Fulton St, Broadway-Nassau St 🚌 M6 ⊘ 8am-4pm ♿ yes

Temple Emanu-El (2, K6)

The world's largest reformed Jewish synagogue is notable for its Byzantine and Near Eastern architecture.

✉ 1 E 65th St at 5th Ave ☎ 744-1400 ℮ www.emanuelnyc .org Ⓔ Lexington Ave (B, Q), 66th St-Hunter College 🚌 M1-4 ⊘ 10am-5pm; tours Sun-Fri ♿ yes

Harlem Church Services

Harlem's famous **Abyssinian Baptist Church** (132 W 138th St; 1, A5; ☎ 862-7474) has a charismatic pastor and a superb choir. Sunday services start at 9am and 11am and last up to two hours. **Canaan Baptist Church** (132 W 116th St; 1, E5; ☎ 866-0301) might be Harlem's friendliest church. The Sunday service is at 10:45am (10am in summer).

Other Harlem churches welcome respectful visitors. Remember to dress neatly, be on time (and stay till the end) and leave your camera in your bag.

PARKS & GARDENS

For a city with a concrete jungle reputation, New York has loads of open space. Some of it's even green. And sometimes you're even allowed on the lawns. Because many residents live in tiny apartments, public parks are highly valued.

Battery Park (3, O5)
Named for the cannons that once protected the harbor, this park offers wonderful water views and often hosts musical events. Peter Minuit Plaza, at the eastern exit of the park, is reputedly the place where the Dutch purchased Manhattan from Native Americans.
✉ Broadway at Battery Pl Ⓜ South Ferry, Bowling Green 🚌 M6, M15 ♿ yes

Esbin-Anderson Photography
Apple-blossom season in the Big Apple

Brooklyn Botanic Garden (6, G2)
This 52-acre haven includes conservatories, a fragrance garden, a meditation area and a path with celebrity handprints (Marianne Moore, Harvey Keitel, Woody Guthrie, Judge Judy). Even with all the rules and regulations (shoes on, no picnics, no blankets), this is a beautiful spot. Kids can get good and dirty in the hands-on Discovery Garden (p. 41).
✉ 1000 Washington Ave btw Eastern Pkwy & Empire Blvd (in Prospect Park), Brooklyn ☎ 718-622-4433 e www.bbg.org Ⓜ Eastern Pkwy-Brooklyn Museum 🚌 B41 🕘 Tues-Fri 8am-6pm, Sat-Sun 10am-6pm (closes 1½hrs earlier Oct-Mar) $ $3/free; free Tues & Sat till noon ♿ yes

Bryant Park (2, O6)
Claim a marble bench or folding chair and crack open a book from the library (p. 22) next door. The Crystal Palace was built here in 1853 but burned down fast in 1858, supposedly by spontaneous combustion. Free film screenings take place Monday night in summer.
✉ 42nd St Ⓜ 42nd St-Grand Central 🚌 M42 🕘 6am-dusk ♿ yes

Neil Setchfield
Whiling away an afternoon in Midtown's Bryant Park

Conservatory Garden

(2, B6) Though it's in Central Park, this pretty, gated garden is still a hideaway. You'll find flowers in bloom most of the year, peaceful lily ponds, trellised roses and plenty of secluded benches where you can sit down with a book, a sketch pad or an amour.
✉ 5th Ave at 105th St 🚇 103rd St (6) 🚌 M1-4 ⏰ 8am-dusk ♿ yes

Greenacre Park

(2, M8) This tiny park is backed by a crashingly noisy waterfall, which somehow manages to be soothing. The tables make this a good place to read the newspaper or catch your breath after walking the Midtown streets.
✉ 221 E 51st St btw 2nd & 3rd Aves 🚇 51st St (6), Lexington Ave (E, F) 🚌 M50, M101-3 ⏰ 8am-8pm ♿ yes

New York Botanical Garden

(4, A2) The 250-acre complex features a Victorian conservatory, a fine rose garden, and a rock garden and museum. Tram, golf-cart or guided walking tours focus on various kinds of plants and birds.
✉ 200th St at Kazimiroff Blvd, the Bronx ☎ 718-817-8700 💻 www.nybg.org 🚇 Bedford Pk Blvd, then bus BX26 🚉 MetroNorth from Grand Central ⏰ Tues-Sun 10am-6pm (closes 2hrs earlier Nov-Mar) 💲 $3/1-2 ♿ yes

Prospect Park

(6, G2) Smaller and calmer than Central Park (but built by the same designers), this park includes a lake and boathouse, an ice-skating rink and the art deco Brooklyn Public Library. Kids can explore the children's historic house museum, visit the animals at the small zoo or take a spin on the carousel.
✉ Flatbush Ave at Grand Army Plaza, Brooklyn ☎ 718-965-8951 💻 www.prospectpark.org 🚇 Grand Army Plaza, Prospect Park 🚌 B41 ⏰ 6am-1am ♿ yes

Wave Hill

(5, C2) Choose a fine day to visit this Victorian house (1843) and its 28 acres of lovely grounds overlooking the Hudson River. Mark Twain and Theodore Roosevelt once lived here. As well as art exhibitions, Wave Hill features weekend family art sessions with materials supplied. Eat at the onsite café or pack a picnic.
✉ W 249th St at Independence Ave, Riverdale, the Bronx ☎ 718-549-3200 💻 www.wavehill.org 🚇 207th St (A), then bus No 7; 231st St (1), then bus No 7 to 252nd St 🚉 MetroNorth from Grand Central to Riverdale 🚌 Bx7, Bx10; Liberty Lines (☎ 718-652-8400) BxM 1 or 2 to 252nd St ⏰ Tues-Sun 9am-5:30pm (closes 4:30pm winter, later Wed in summer) 💲 $4/2, children under 6 free; free all day Tues & Sat till noon, free Nov-Mar ♿ yes

Off the Beaten Track

New York's tracks are beaten down pretty flat, but it's still possible to find places that, though not exactly undiscovered, aren't crawling with people. On the island, try **Conservatory Garden** (above) and **Greenacre Park** (above). Often all you need to do to leave the hordes behind is get out of Manhattan. In the outlying boroughs, head to the **Isamu Noguchi Garden Museum** (p. 32), **Jacques Marchais Center of Tibetan Art** (p. 32) and **Wave Hill** (above).

Tibetan prayer flags fly at the Jacques Marchais Center.

NEW YORK CITY FOR CHILDREN

With its abundance of world-famous sites, tours and attractions, New York is an ideal place to bring children. Several museums are dedicated to the younger set, and many annual events appeal to kids. The Big Apple Circus visits Lincoln Center each winter.

Look for the ♣ elsewhere in the book to find other kid-friendly places. *New York Family* is a free monthly newspaper full of kid-friendly events.

Bronx Zoo (4, A3)

One of the biggest and best zoos anywhere boasts over 6000 animals, 265 acres of naturalistic enclosures, a kid's zoo (April-October) and a zeal for conservation. The Bengali Express, a monorail trip through 'Asia' (May-October), and the Congo Forest are worth the extra cost.

✉ Fordham Rd at Bronx River Pkwy, the Bronx ☎ 718-367-1010 ℮ www.wcs.org ⊖ Pelham Pkwy (2), E 180th St (5) 🚇 Metro-North Getaway packages (☎ 532-4900) 🚌 Liberty Lines BxM11 Express from Madison Ave 🚗 Exit 6 from Bronx River Pkwy ⊙ 10am-5pm (Sat-Sun & holidays to 5:30pm, Nov-Mar to 4:30pm) ⑤ $9/5; free Wed ⴲ yes

Children's Museum of the Arts (3, J6)

If being dragged around the Soho galleries has inspired your kids, let them loose here. They can draw, paint, make music and join workshops (good for ages 10 months to 10 years).

✉ 182 Lafayette St at Broome St ☎ 274-0986 ℮ www.cmany.org ⊖ Spring St (6) 🚌 M103 ⊙ Wed-Sun noon-5pm (Thurs to 6pm) ⑤ $5

Stars in the making at the Children's Museum

Angus Oborn

Children's Museum of Manhattan (2, G2)

Toddlers can put their hands all over the discovery centers, and older, techno-logically savvy kids can work in a TV studio. The museum also runs crafts workshops on weekends.

✉ 212 W 83rd St at Amsterdam Ave ☎ 721-1234 ℮ www.cmom.org ⊖ 79th St (1, 9) 🚌 M7, M11 ⊙ Wed-Sun 10am-5pm (extended summer hrs) ⑤ $6/3 ⴲ yes

Madame Tussaud's Wax Museum (2, O4)

The silly, overpriced but fun wax museum features 200 models of local figures like Frank Sinatra, Yoko Ono and Woody Allen, along with Princess Diana and gory French revolution scenes.

✉ 234 W 42nd St btw 7th & 8th Aves ☎ 800-246-8872 ℮ www.madame-tussauds.com ⊖ 42nd St-Times Square ⊙ 10am-8pm ⑤ $20/16-18, children under 4 free ⴲ yes

Little Green Thumbs

The amazing **Children's Adventure Garden** at the New York Botanical Garden (p. 40) includes a Sun, Dirt and Water Gallery, a wetland trail and a Boulder Maze.

The **Discovery Garden** at the Brooklyn Botanic Garden (p. 39) is a place kids and grownups can explore together; there's a special area for toddlers. The adjoining **Children's Garden** has given more than 20,000 children the opportunity to plant, tend and reap flowers, plants and vegetables.

New York Aquarium

(6, K4) Over 8000 specimens from 350 species make for a full watery world. The perfect place for young children, the aquarium boasts a touch pool bursting with small forms of sea life, including starfish. Marine mammals show their stuff in the aquarium's amphitheater – the bottlenose dolphins are the stars from May to October. Kids can also catch an underwater glimpse of whales and seals through the observation windows.
✉ **Surf Ave at W 8th St, Coney Island, Brooklyn** ☎ **718-265-3474** e **www .nyaquarium.org** ⊕ W 8th St-NY Aquarium ⏰ 10am-4:30pm ⑨ $9.75/6 ♿ yes

New York Hall of Science (6, B4)

Dedicated to science and technology, this place specializes in hands-on exhibits where kids can make water flow upward, watch tarantulas eat crickets or hang out on a 3-D spider web. Activities should suit a range of ages, whether your curious kid's a precocious preschooler or an adolescent astronomer.
✉ **111th St at 47th Ave, Corona, Queens** ☎ **718-699-0005** e **www.nyhallsci.org** ⊕ 111th St (7) ⏰ Mon-Wed 9:30am-2pm, Thurs-Sun 9:30am-5pm (extended summer hrs) ⑨ $7.50/5; free Thurs & Fri 2-5pm (except in summer); Science Playground $2 ♿ yes

PlaySpace (2, E3)

The perfect place for rainy or sweltering afternoons, this indoor playground features a treehouse, sandbox, slides, climbing frames, dress-ups and room just to run around shrieking. It's good for ages six months to six years.
✉ **2473 Broadway at 92nd St** ☎ **769-2300** ⊕ 96th St (1, 2, 3, 9) 🚌 M104 ⏰ 10am-5:30pm ⑨ $7.50 ♿ yes

Sony Wonder (2, L6)

Sure, it's going to make your kids Sony fans, but this free Technology Lab is worth a look – the talking robot is amazing. Go in the afternoon to avoid school groups.
✉ **550 Madison Ave at 55th St** ☎ **833-8100** e **wondertechlab .sony.com** ⊕ 51st St (6), 5th Ave (E, F), 59th St (4, 5, 6) 🚌 M1-5, M57 ⏰ Tues-Sat 10am-6pm (Thurs to 8pm), Sun noon-6pm ⑨ free

Staten Island Children's Museum

(4, E2) At this museum of discovery and fun, kids can get puzzled, get active and sometimes get messy doing anything from watching insects being born to exploring a pirate ship to inventing a play.
✉ **Snug Harbor Cultural Center, 1000 Richmond Terrace, Staten Island** ☎ **718-273-2060** e **www.snug-harbor .org** 🚌 S40 from Staten Island Ferry Terminal ⏰ Tues-Sun noon-5pm (June-Sept Tues-Sun from 11am) ⑨ $4, children under 2 free, seniors free Wed ♿ yes

Babysitting & Child Care

Nannies and babysitters are happy to come to hotels or private homes to look after your children. Fees start at $12/hr plus an agency fee of about $25, and there's usually a four-hour minimum. Though agencies appreciate a day's notice, they're usually able to find someone at the last minute. **Best Domestic Services Agency** (☎ 685-0351) and **Professional Nannies** (☎ 692-9510) are reputable agencies.

Tot traffic: even the kids in NYC move fast.

Edwin-Anderson Photography

QUIRKY NEW YORK

Evolution (3, H5)
Fancy a raccoon penis? A tarantula? Giraffe hair bracelet? Insects, bones, fossils, eggs, teeth and lots of icky things in jars – this natural history shop certainly has an eye on the weird prize.

✉ **120 Spring St at Mercer St** ☎ **343-1114**
📧 **www.evolutionnyc.com** 🚇 **Spring St (6)**
🕐 **11am-7pm**

Red-light district

Galapagos (6, E2)
Skirt the reflecting pool to this roomy bar where you can see two trapeze artists who sing kooky country songs, plus hula hoopers, bands, theater and movie screenings with an interesting, arty crowd.

✉ **70 N 6th St, Williamsburg, Brooklyn**
☎ **718-782-5188**
📧 **www.galapagosart space.com** 🚇 **Bedford Ave** 🕐 **6pm-2am (Fri-Sat to 4am)** 💲 **main room free, backroom $5-10**

La Nouvelle Justine
(3, G7) Foot worship with your martini? Doggy obedience training with that beer? S&M is on the menu,

from the baby food (served in a high chair) to the chocolate stiletto for dessert. Afterward, take yourself to Lucky Cheng's (24 1st Ave; ☎ 473-0516), around the corner, for drag waitresses and camp karaoke.

✉ **101 E 2nd St at 1st Ave** ☎ **673-8908**
📧 **www.lanouvelle justine.com** 🚇 **2nd Ave**
🚌 **M15** 🕐 **6pm-1am (Fri-Sat to 4am)**

Mermaid Parade
(6, K4) Coney Island's shore is swamped by mermaids, mer-fellas and assorted cheerful freaks emerging in their dress-ups from the lagoons of

Gotham. It's a fun day, attracting everyone from sparkly kids to spangled drag queens.

✉ **Surf Ave, Coney Island, Brooklyn**
🚇 **Coney Island-Stillwell Ave** 🕐 **Sun 1pm, late June-early Jul**

Rico Cafe (3, F9)
This hookah lounge is a Middle Eastern mirage in Alphabet City. Pack a pipe to have with your coffee and cake, and it's easy to pretend you've got a team of camels waiting outside to take you back to the souk.

✉ **153 Ave C btw 9th & 10th Sts** ☎ **505-5757**
🚇 **1st Ave** 🚌 **M15**
🕐 **7am-5am** 💲 **$7**

Walks on the Wild Side
Have a wacky day in New York by fitting in the following:

- techno tenpin bowling at **Bowlmor Lanes** (p. 96)
- taking a stroll through the freakish **Coney Island Circus Sideshow** (p. 50)
- visiting Peter Beard's visceral, epic, objectionable installation **The Time Is Always Now** (476 Broome St; 3, J5; ☎ 343-2424) – Africa, blood and pretty women
- downing a midnight mojito at **Milk & Honey** (134 Eldridge St; 3, J7; ☎ 625-3397), a 'secret' bar that requires reservations

Bowlmor: retro bowling in the Village

KEEPING FIT

Gyms

Even mid-range hotels have small fitness centers these days, and some of the fancier hotels offer excellent training facilities. Otherwise, gyms all over the city sell day passes, usually for about $20.

Running

Believe it or not, Manhattan has three traffic-free spots: Central Park's 6.2-mile roadway, which loops around the park (closed to cars Mon-Fri 10am-3pm & 7-10pm, Jan to late Nov, and 7pm Fri to 6am Mon year-round); the soft 1-mile path that encircles the Jacqueline Kennedy Onassis Reservoir; and the Hudson River path (Battery Park to 125th St), which offers great views of the Statue of Liberty and the Jersey Shore. The **New York Road Runners Club** (☎ 860-4455) organizes regular runs around the city.

Skating

Show off your inline skating skills (or lack thereof) at Central Park, on the mall that runs east of Sheep Meadow. If you're just starting out, rent a pair of wheels from nearby **Blades West** (120 W 72nd St; 2, H3; ☎ 787-3911).

The Chelsea Piers complex has roller rinks and ramps, and the path along the Hudson between Battery Park and 125th St goes right by here.

Swimming

Much of the swimming done in New York happens in expensive private clubs, but 50 free city pools open up in summer. Some pools set aside lap swimming times; the rest of the time, they tend to be taken over by dive-bombing kids. For a list of pools, see the Government Listings in the white pages of the phone book (under 'New York City Offices, Parks & Recreation').

Yoga

Yoga is extremely popular in New York. Not only are there a lot of people wanting to align those pesky chakras, but it's also a low-impact way of toning up and chilling out.

Never a dull moment: recreation rush hour in Central Park

Greg Gawlowski

Asser Levy Bath

(3, D8) The pleasant 23yd (25m) pool offers lap swimming weekdays 7-8:30am and 7-8:30pm in summer. A less appealing indoor pool operates in winter. There's a small gym on the premises, too.
✉ E 23rd St at Asser Levy Pl ☎ 447-2020 Ⓔ 1st Ave 🚌 M16, M21, M23 ⏱ June-Aug Mon-Fri 6:30am-8:30pm, Sat-Sun 8am-7:30pm Ⓢ free

Chelsea Piers

(3, D1) This massive gym has a thousand ways to make you sweat. Choose – if you can – from bowling, skating, horseback-riding, indoor rockwall-climbing and swinging a golf club.
✉ 23rd St at Hudson River ☎ 336-6000 e www.chelseapiers.com Ⓔ 23rd St (C, E) 🚌 M14, M23 ⏱ gym Mon-Fri 6am-11pm, Sat-Sun 8am-9pm Ⓢ $50/day ♿ yes

Downtown Boathouse

(3, K3; 3, C1) From May to early fall, try free walk-up kayaking at two sheltered embayments on the Hudson – you'll get wet, so bring a change of clothes. Experienced kayakers can sometimes join trips to the Statue of Liberty; call for information.
✉ Pier 26, Hudson River at Hubert St; Pier 64, Hudson River at 24th St ☎ 385-8169 e www.downtown boathouse.org Ⓔ Pier 26: Chambers St (1, 2, 3, 9), Canal St (2, 3); Pier 64: 23rd St (C, E) ⏱ Pier 26: Sat-Sun 9am-6pm, Pier 24: Sat-Sun 9am-4pm Ⓢ free

Working up a sweat on the Chelsea Piers

New York Integral Yoga Institute (3, E4)

Beginners, experts and everyone in between can join meditation programs and yoga classes. The instructors request that you bring a towel, wear clean socks and don't eat for 2hrs before class. Afterward, replenish at the great whole-food supermarket downstairs.
✉ 227 W 13th St btw 7th & 8th Aves ☎ 929-0586 e www.integral yogaofnewyork.org Ⓔ 14th St (1, 2, 3, 9, A, C, E), 8th Ave Ⓢ most classes $11 for 85mins; 1wk unlimited classes $45

Soho Sanctuary

(3, H5) Enjoy the pampering vibe at this women-only day spa, which offers massage (including reflexology and shiatsu), facials,

aromatherapy and yoga and Alexander Technique sessions.
✉ 3rd fl, 119 Mercer St btw Prince & Spring Sts ☎ 334-5550 Ⓔ Spring St (6) ⏱ Tues-Fri 10am-9pm, Sat 10am-6pm, Sun noon-6pm Ⓢ drop-in yoga class $20, 1hr massage or facial $95

Tenth St Baths (3, F7)

Younger local residents mix with grizzled regulars at these historic steam baths. Go for steam and sauna or try a Russian-style massage, Dead Sea Salt Scrub or mud treatment.
✉ 268 E 10th St btw Ave A & 1st Ave ☎ 674-9250 Ⓔ 1st Ave ⏱ 11am-10pm (ladies only Wed 9am-2pm, men only Sun 7:30am-2pm) Ⓢ $22, 1hr massage $60 ♿ no

Scoring with the Locals

New Yorkers are often happy to let visitors join in their informal sports. Head to **Prospect Park** (6, G2) on summer weekends for Frisbee free-for-alls. If you know your bishop from your elbow, play lightning-fast chess in **Washington Square Park** (3, G5).

Playground basketball games offer a good way to let off 9-to-5 steam. For young hotshots, there's also the hope that a tarmac-prowling college scout will spot them. The **courts at W 4th St & 6th Ave** (3, G4) are great for watching high-quality hoops.

out & about

WALKING TOURS
Central Park

From Columbus Circle ❶, go through Merchants' Gate ❷ and up to Sheep Meadow ❸, a green expanse favored by sunbathers and frolickers. Turn right onto a pathway that runs along the southern side of the meadow to the Carousel ❹ and the Dairy ❺, where the park's visitors' center is located.

Bethesda Fountain: a park focal point

North of the Dairy, beyond the Christopher Columbus statue, is the Mall ❻, bordered by 150 American elms. At the end of the Mall, you'll see Bethesda Fountain ❼, a hippie

> **distance** 2.8 miles (5km)
> **duration** 2hrs
> ▶ **start** Columbus Circle subway
> ● **end** 72nd St subway (B, C)

hangout in the 1960s. Continue on the path to the left to the Bow Bridge ❽. Cross the bridge to the Ramble ❾, a lush, wooded expanse where dog owners congregate. Turn right to stop for a meal or drink at Park View at the Boathouse ❿, overlooking the lake.

At its north end, the Ramble leads to Belvedere Castle ⓫ and the Delacorte Theater ⓬, where the Joseph Papp Public Theater puts on free performances in summer. Immediately beyond is the Great Lawn ⓭, a group of softball fields where the New York Philharmonic and Metropolitan Opera play each summer.

Turning left and walking down West Dr to 72nd St brings you to Strawberry Fields ⓮, dedicated to John Lennon, who lived nearby.

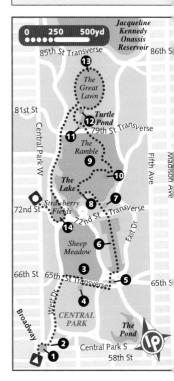

Chinatown

Though Chinese traders first arrived in the 1780s, New York's community numbered only 150 by 1859. There were three major growth spurts: when overlanders came from California in the 1870s, when the Chinese Exclusion Act was repealed in 1943 and when immigration quotas were relaxed in 1968. Today, Chinatown is a thriving pan-Asian community of 120,000.

The walk starts at Chatham Square ➊, where the goods of Irish debtors were auctioned off in the early 19th century. Walk up Doyers St, the oldest street in Chinatown, and turn left onto Pell St, named for a butcher who worked here in the colonial period. Cross Mott St to the Church of the Transfiguration ➋, at No 29, once an Irish and Italian church. North on Mott St, you'll pass the quenching Saint's Alp Teahouse ➌, at No 51. Turn left on Bayard St to find the Museum of Chinese in the Americas ➍. The delicious food stop Pho Viet Huong ➎ is across Mulberry St.

Double back and continue north on Mott. The Eastern States Buddhist Temple ➏ is at No 64 – stop for a $1 fortune. Turn left on Canal St and follow it to Broadway, browsing at the shop Pearl River ➐, No 277, on the way. Alternatively, turn right on Canal St and cross the Bowery to Mahayana Buddhist Temple ➑, No 133, to see the huge Buddha inside. A pedestrian path recently opened over the Manhattan Bridge ➒ and begins right over Canal St – about a mile later, you'll end up in Flatbush Ave, downtown Brooklyn.

SIGHTS & HIGHLIGHTS

Saint's Alp Teahouse (p. 71)
Museum of Chinese in the Americas (p. 33)
Pho Viet Huong (p. 71)
Pearl River (p. 57)

Pedal power in Chinatown

Robert Reid

---

distance 1-1.5 miles (1.5-2.5km)   **duration** 1½hrs
▶ **start** M9, M15, M22 bus stop
⬤ **end** Manhattan: Canal St subway (N, R); Brooklyn: York St subway (F)

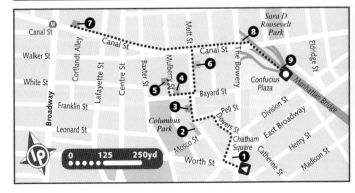

Greenwich Village

From Washington Square Park ❶, head down Thompson St past Judson Memorial Church ❷, designed by Stanford White. Cross W 3rd St and see chess shops ❸ on the left. Turn right at Bleecker St to Le Figaro ❹, No 184, a café where Jack Kerouac and Allen Ginsberg hung out. Turn right up MacDougal St and pay homage at Café Wha? ❺, No 115 – Jimi Hendrix played here. Duck down Minetta Lane, turn left into Minetta St and then right onto 6th Ave.

Walk up to W 4th St, stopping off at the basketball courts ❻. Cross 6th Ave to 161 W 4th St ❼ – Bob Dylan lived here in the early 1960s. Walk down cute Cornelia St to Bleecker St, turn right and head to 7th Ave. Cross over and veer into Commerce St. Turning right at Bedford St brings you to New York's narrowest house ❽, No 75½, past the home of Edna St Vincent Millay. Detour up Barrow St to Federal row houses ❾ at Nos 49 and 51. Continue along Bedford St to Chumley's ❿, No 86, for pub meals and speakeasy atmosphere. Farther along Bedford, duck left on Grove St to see more lovely row houses ⓫. Bedford St comes to an end at Christopher St, the artery of gay life in the Village. Turn right and walk up to Stonewall Place ⓬.

SIGHTS & HIGHLIGHTS

Washington Square Park
Chumley's (p. 96)
Stonewall Place (p. 98)

Pieces of the past for sale in the Village

---

distance 2.6 miles (4km) **duration** 2hrs
▶ **start** W 4th St subway
● **end** Christopher St subway

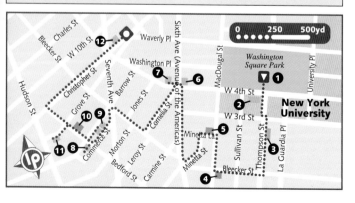

EXCURSIONS
City Island   (5, C2)

This New England–style pocket in, of all places, the Bronx makes a great getaway. The island juts into Long Island Sound, with a cause-way connecting it to the mainland. You won't see much boat-building and fishing here these days, but the clapboard cottages and waterside seafood joints can make for a very un–New York breather, especially during the week. The City Island Art Organization (278 City Island Ave; ☎ 718-885-9316) can clue you in on the island's art stops. Numerous quaint and quirky shops keep the retail trade alive.

White-picket fences and flags complete the old-fashioned cottage look.

Cold Spring   (5, B2)

Cold Spring, a quaint village on the eastern bank of the Hudson River 90 minutes north of New York, abounds with antique shops, inns and restaurants. A lovely destination in itself, it makes a good base for walks along the river and into the countryside. The steep Washburn Trail to the top of Mt Taurus is the best mix of challenge and terrific scenery. Tours of the Rockefeller Estate, called Kykuit (Route 9, Sleepy Hollow; ☎ 914-631-6141; May-Nov Wed-Mon 10am-3pm; $20/17-19), take in spectacular grounds and the art-stuffed mansion.

Cold Spring is particularly enjoyable in autumn, when the leaves are turning. Pick up self-guided walking tour brochures in town shops.

Coney Island (5, C2)

Home of the amusement park Dreamland, this summer playground has long attracted sweating city dwellers to its fun house, sideshow games and bumper car rides. In the pre-WWI heyday, 'amusements' included elephants on water slides and warm jets of air blown up from the walkways to raise women's skirts. These days, the 'island' is still worth a trip: the Cyclone roller coaster is truly terrifying (including a 100ft plunge at almost 70mph) and the Circus Sideshow (Surf Ave & W 12th St; ☎ 718-372-5159; June-Aug Sat-Sun 1-10pm; $5/3) is freak-abulous.

The Brooklyn Cyclones (☎ 718-449-8497) baseball field opened in 2001, and the trash-art Mermaid Parade (p. 43) kicks off here in June. Even in winter, when everything's shut, the boardwalk stroll to Russian enclave Brighton Beach is appealing.

Thrills 'n' chills

Princeton (5, D1)

Best known for its Ivy League university, which educates 6000 students per year, Princeton is also a historic place, the site of an important Revolutionary War battle on January 3, 1777, and an erstwhile national capital (four months in 1783). The Princeton Battlefield State Park, where the famous skirmish ended in a decisive victory for George Washington, has remained virtually unchanged – an illustrated plan of the fighting stands next to the flagpole.

You can take a stroll by Albert Einstein's Home (112 Mercer St), but you're not allowed inside. Princeton boasts some lovely architecture, including the Gothic marvels of the university, and a nice array of shops and restaurants along Nassau and Witherspoon Sts.

ORGANIZED TOURS

Arthur Marks

A colorful character who's tailored tours for 36 years sings his way through the city. For an anecdotal tour of Greenwich Village or an architectural tour of Tribeca, Arthur could be your man.

✉ **24 5th Ave, New York, NY 10011** ☎ **673-0477** ⑨ **negotiable from $400 for 2½hrs (1-40 people)**

Big Onion Walking Tours

Cheerfully obsessed historians, many of them PhD candidates, lead tours with themes like immigrant New York, the Jewish Lower East Side, gay and lesbian history, New York's 'Victorian City of the Dead' and multiethnic eating 'from Naples to Bialystok to Beijing.'

☎ **439-1090** 🅔 **www.bigonion.com** ⑨ **$12-18**

Circle Line (2, O1)

One popular 3hr tour circumnavigates Manhattan and cruises close to the Statue of Liberty. The sunset Harbor Lights tour is shorter, while The Beast ride puts wind in your hair. Circle Line also offers special fall foliage cruises up the scenic Hudson Valley in October.

✉ **Pier 83, W 42nd St at 12th Ave** ☎ **563-3200** 🅔 **www.circle line.com** ☺ **island tours hourly on the half-hour 9:30am-4:30pm (no tour at 11:30am), Harbor Lights 7pm** ⑨ **full island $24/10, Harbor Lights $20/17/10**

Gangland Tours

(3, H8) True crime fans love this tour of the underworld haunts of criminal characters. The 2hr trip is most atmospheric at night.

✉ **depart Lansky Lounge, 104 Norfolk St at Delancey St** ☎ **334-0492** 🅔 **www.gang landtours.com** ☺ **Mon-Thurs 8:30pm, Sat 11am, Sun 10am & 8:30pm** ⑨ **$85**

Harlem Jazz Tour

(2, M4) Dana Jackson's stretch-limo trips to Harlem jazz jams eliminate the problem of snaring a 'tween-club cab. He might even introduce you to the musicians.

✉ **depart Starbucks, 325 W 49th St btw 8th & 9th Aves** ☎ **765-2114** 🅔 **limotour@ rcn.com** ☺ **9pm-1am** ⑨ **$35-70**

Helicopter Flight Services (3, O5; 3, B1)

The New Yorker tour spins around the Statue of Liberty and Manhattan as far as Central Park; the pricier Ultimate tour includes Yankee Stadium.

✉ **Downtown Manhattan Heliport, South St; Hudson River Heliport, W 30th St at 12th Ave** ☎ **355-0801** 🅔 **www.heliny.com** ☺ **Downtown Manhattan Heliport Mon-Fri 9am-6:30pm, Hudson River Heliport Sat-Sun 11am-6pm** ⑨ **$99-139**

Jazz 'n' Blues Floater

Circle Line (☎ 630-8888) hosts jazz, blues and funk music cruises from May to September, with top artists and twinkling harbor lights. James Cotton, Buckwheat Zydeco and The Iguanas have all performed recently. Call to see who's been snagged for the current season; tickets are around $35.

Kim Grant

All aboard!

Howard Goldberg's Adventure on a Shoestring

Howard's weekend tours include Haunted Greenwich Village, Marilyn Monroe's Manhattan and Elegant Gramercy Park; all take you off the tourist lemming trail.
☎ 265-2663 ⑤ $5

Joyce Gold History Tours of New York

This university history teacher leads a varied program of Manhattan walking tours geared toward serious history buffs and those interested in the quirky and scandalous.
✉ 141 W 17th St, New York, NY 10011
☎ 242-5762 e www.nyctours.com ⑤ $12

Kenny Kramer (2, O3)

If reruns aren't enough, join the K-man for 3hrs of *Seinfeld* background, trivia and gossip. The real-life inspiration for the TV character hosts this weekend-only bus tour (but don't worry — you won't be riding around town on the yellow school bus that the TV Kramer used for his J Peterman tours).
✉ depart Pulse Theater, 432 W 42nd St btw 9th & 10th Aves
☎ 268-5525
e www.kennykramer.com ⑤ $37.50

NY Waterway (2, O2)

Though commuter ferries are good for a glance at the Statue, there's nothing like a cruise for photo ops aplenty. NY Waterway will even drop you at a baseball game.
✉ Pier 78, W 38th St at 12th Ave ☎ 800-533-3779 e www.nywaterway.com
⑤ $19/9 for 90mins; prices vary

On Location Tours

(2, O5) Scope out locations and get behind-the-scenes gossip about *Seinfeld, Friends, NYPD Blue, Mad About You* and *Sex and the City* on this Manhattan bus tour. Sunday's all-*Sopranos* version comes complete with Mafia lingo.
☎ 334-0492, 935-0168
e www.sceneontv.com ⑤ $20-30/10, children under 5 free

Radical Walking Tours

Bruce Kayton's alternative history tours cover Greenwich Village (try Radical Lovers or Riots, Murders & Prohibition), plus Harlem and Wall St (Money & Other Evils). You can learn about everything from New York's first organized slave revolt to the history of condoms.
☎ 718-492-0069
e www.he.net/~radtours ⊙ Mar-Dec
⑤ $10

World Yacht (2, O2)

You've got to dress up for these well-regarded culinary cruises and dinner dances around Manhattan. Top chefs craft the meals. Reservations required.
✉ depart Pier 81, W 41st St at 12th Ave
☎ 630-8100 e www.worldyacht.com
⑤ $42 for 2hr brunch, $67-79 for 3hr dinner

Classic Architecture

As Americans sought to define their new nation, they looked to the ancient societies of Greece and Rome for examples to emulate. Classical architecture, it was felt, gave expression to the aspirations of the young republic. Build on your architectural knowledge by taking a Municipal Arts Society (☎ 935-3960) tour, which leaves from Grand Central Terminal's main concourse on Wednesday at 12:30pm.

A beaux arts gem: Grand Central Terminal

shopping

From world-famous stores to quirky back-street shops, there's no beating New York for range and quality. And while it may not be strictly true that you can find 'anything' in the Apple, it is pleasingly difficult to come up with an acquisitive craving that can't be satisfied. Tibetan fur-rimmed hat? Absolutely. Worm-studded lollypops? Thought you'd never ask!

In fact, the shopping is so good that you might find yourself hunting for something you only realize you need when it's time to depart: extra luggage to transport your goodies home.

Shopping Areas

Department, chain and theme stores populate **Midtown**, particularly **5th Ave** and the more upscale **Madison Ave**. Farther north, Madison becomes more exclusive yet, with ritzy boutiques and antiques emporiums. The **Garment District** (7th Ave btw 34th & 42nd Sts) is full of clothing wholesalers and sample sales.

Greenwich Village features thrift stores and a shoe and leather strip (8th St between 5th and 6th Aves). Funky little stores dot the **East Village** (try 7th, 8th and 9th Sts between Ave A and 3rd Ave).

Soho has lost its edge of late, with mainstream and uptown stores infiltrating. Still, designers like Nicole Miller (p. 57) bring attitude and class to the 'hood. Up-and-coming designers cluster in **Nolita**, to the east.

Orchard St, on the **Lower East Side**, is the spot for inexpensive luggage and leather clothing. Sunday is the big shopping day; most shops are closed on Friday afternoon and all day Saturday while their owners observe the Jewish Sabbath. The merchants association (261 Broome St; 3, J8; ☎ 226-9010) produces a walking tour leaflet.

Chinatown is an assault on the senses – you can buy a gorgeous silk waistcoat, medicinal bark and a crispy duck without even hunting. Grand, Canal and Mulberry Sts boast the most interesting shops.

Flea Markets
Weekend markets make for easy browsing and good buys.

- **Annex Antiques Fair & Flea Market** (6th Ave at W 26th St; 3, C4)
- **Grand St Antiques Fair** (Broadway at Grand St; 3, J6)
- **Greenflea Markets** (67th St btw 1st & York Aves; 2, J8; Sat only; also at Columbus Ave btw 76th & 77th Sts; 2, G4; Sun only)
- **Weekend market** (Ave A at 11th St; 3, F8)

Angus Oborn

New Yorkers clean out their closets.

DEPARTMENT STORES

Barney's (2, K6)
Shirts are called 'shirtings' here, which pretty much sets the tone at this hip and haughty chain store that's famous for treating customers as too fat, too poor and, in the men's department, too straight.
✉ 660 Madison Ave at 61st St ☎ 826-8900 🚇 59th St (4, 5, 6), Lexington Ave (N, R) 🚌 M1-4 ⊙ Mon-Fri 10am-8pm, Sat 10am-7pm, Sun 11am-6pm

Bergdorf Goodman
(2, L6) A favorite stop for out-of-towners looking for classy gifts in prestige wrapping, Bergdorf's features terrific jewelry and couture collections, attentive staff and great sales. The men's wear department is across the street.
✉ 754 5th Ave at 58th St ☎ 753-7300 🚇 5th Ave (N, R), 59th St (4, 5, 6) 🚌 M1-5, M57 ⊙ Mon-Sat 10am-7pm (Thurs to 8pm), Sun noon-6pm

Bloomingdale's
(2, K7) Bloomie's is a cramped, crowded but well-loved New York institution. The addition of snappy young designers has reinvigorated the clothing range in recent years.
✉ E 59th St at Lexington Ave ☎ 705-2000 🚇 59th St (4, 5, 6), Lexington Ave (N, R) ⊙ Mon-Wed 10am-8:30pm, Thurs-Fri 10am-10pm, Sat 10am-8:30pm, Sun 11am-7pm

Century 21 (3, M5)
This discount department store includes a large, if unreliable, selection of men's and women's wear. Whatever it is, it will always be marked down. Shopping here is a ritual for downtown office workers.
✉ 22 Cortlandt St btw Church St & Broadway ☎ 227-9092 🚇 Cortlandt St, Fulton St ⊙ Mon-Fri 7:45am-8pm (Thurs to 8:30pm), Sat 10am-7:30pm, Sun 11am-7pm

Henri Bendel (2, L6)
Check out curious, fun clothing, cosmetics and accessories from newly established and flavor-of-the-moment designers. A warning: the fashion here tends to be so 'now' that it becomes 'yesterday' easily.
✉ 712 5th Ave at 56th St ☎ 247-1100 🚇 5th Ave (E, F, N, R), 57th St (B, Q) 🚌 M1-5 ⊙ Mon-Sat 10am-7pm (Thurs to 8pm), Sun noon-6pm

Lord & Taylor (2, O6)
The ten floors of fashion here tend to favor conservative American daywear for the ladies. Swimsuits are also a strong point. The sales assistants are pleasantly nonthreatening, even in the cosmetics department. No need to beware the spritzers!
✉ 424 5th Ave at 39th St ☎ 391-3344 🚇 42nd St 🚌 M1-5 ⊙ Mon-Tues & Sat 10am-7pm, Wed-Fri 10am-8:30pm, Sun 11am-7pm

Macy's (2, P5)
Though its claim to be the world's largest store is dubious (Moscow's Gum store, among others, would like to hold that title), Macy's is certainly massive. Even so, it's quite easy to manage, except during the big sales, when the crowds turn out. Sponsor of the ever-popular Thanksgiving Day parade, Macy's has earned the affections of fickle New Yorkers.
✉ 151 W 34th St at Broadway ☎ 695-4400 🚇 34th St-Herald Sq ⊙ Mon-Sat 10am-8:30pm, Sun 11am-7pm

Bag ladies (and gentlemen): shoppers on the streets

Angus Oborn

Saks Fifth Ave (2, M6)
Saks has spread everywhere, but its flagship store is right here, as the name suggests. Famous for its January sale, Saks draws shoppers year-round to its vast ground-floor selling space where you'll find pleasantly arranged stock and helpful staff.
✉ **611 5th Ave at 50th St ☎ 753-4000**
🄴 **www.saksfifth avenue.com** 🚇 **Rocke-feller Center** 🚌 **M1-4, M50** 🕐 **Mon-Fri 10am-7pm (Thurs to 8pm), Sat 10am-6:30pm, Sun noon-6pm**

Takashimaya (2, L6)
This stunning, Japanese-owned department store sells goods from all over the world, with an emphasis on style, craftsmanship and gorgeous packaging. Check out the great travel gear upstairs and the botanical gems at the ground-floor florist. Escape the bustle by taking 'East-West afternoon tea' in The Teabox, in the basement.
✉ **693 5th Ave btw 54th & 55th Sts**
☎ **350-0100** 🚇 **5th Ave (E, F, N, R)** 🚌 **M1-4** 🕐 **Mon-Sat 10am-7pm, Sun noon-5pm**

A shopping landmark

CLOTHING

Brooks Brothers
(2, N6) This legendary store sells conservative clothing and formal wear, largely for men, though it also carries a small, immaculate women's range. The fitting rooms are as big as some Manhattan apartments.
✉ **346 Madison Ave at 44th St ☎ 682-8800** 🚇 **42nd St-Grand Central** 🚌 **M1-5** 🕐 **Mon-Sat 9am-7pm (Thurs to 8pm), Sun noon-6pm**

Calvin Klein (2, K6)
The media-savvy designer's flagship store is a study in elegance. Clothes hang arm's length from each other, swinging lazily in a subtle breeze, and sales staff drift around displaying their perfect skin.
✉ **654 Madison Ave at 60th St ☎ 292-9000** 🚇 **59th St (4, 5, 6), 5th Ave (N, R)** 🚌 **M1-4** 🕐 **Mon-Sat 10am-7pm (Thurs to 8pm), Sun noon-6pm**

Calypso (3, H6)
This Nolita pioneer has become something of a mini-empire, but the clothes – from slinky to cute and flouncy to cozy – are as colorful and stylish as ever. Parents can dress their kids at Calypso Enfant i Bebe (426 Broome St).
✉ **280 Mott St at Houston St ☎ 965-0990** 🚇 **Broadway-Lafayette St, Spring St (6), 2nd Ave** 🚌 **M21**

🕐 **Mon-Fri 11am-7pm, Sat 11am-7:30pm, Sun noon-6pm**

Canal Jean Co (3, J6)
Brand-name living comes at easy prices at this massive shop, with vintage in the bargain basement and casual wear up top.
✉ **504 Broadway btw Spring & Broome Sts**
☎ **226-1130** 🚇 **Spring St (6)** 🕐 **9:30am-9pm**

Outlets, Markdowns, Bargains
Bargain hunting? Try **Find Outlet** (229 Mott St btw Prince & Spring Sts; 3, H6; ☎ 226-5167), which carries women's fashion. **Daffy's** (25 E 57th St at 5th Ave; 2, L6; ☎ 376-4477) sells marked-down (and mostly dressed-down) clothing, including designer samples and kids' clothes. Some items are 75% off. Look for high-fashion knockoffs along E 8th St between Broadway and 6th Ave.

Elysa Lazar is New York's shopping czar – her *Sales & Bargain Report* (🄴 www.lazarshopping .com) is only available by subscription, though you can order just one issue. *Time Out New York* also lists sample sales.

Diane von Fürstenberg (3, F2)
Famous in the 1970s for her classic wrap dress, now updated in printed silk, von Fürstenberg also offers a full line of slinky separates. The performance space here is often used for parties.
✉ 385 W 12th St btw Washington & West Sts
☎ 646-486-4800
🚇 14th St-8th Ave
🚌 M14 ⏰ Mon-Fri 11am-7pm (Thurs to 8pm), Sat 11am-6pm, Sun noon-5pm

Final Home (3, H6)
Ex-Issey Miyake designer Kosuke Tsumura's mostly male streetwear was inspired by the plight of the homeless. The street people with $300 to spend on a rain jacket covered in zippers and 50 pockets must be very happy. DJs spin tunes in the cool store.
✉ 241 Lafayette St btw Prince & Spring Sts
☎ 966-0202 🚇 Spring St (6), Prince St
⏰ Mon-Sat 11am-7pm, Sun noon-6pm

Fiorucci (3, H6)
After a decade-long absence from New York, the Milan fashion house Fiorucci has returned. The old Fiorucci attracted everyone from Jackie O to Madonna, but this extravagant new store is a bit more mainstream, with hippie chic and trash-cherub wearables tabled among classy white columns. You might spot a model or two in the onsite café, which offers (surprise, surprise) Italian fare.
✉ 622 Broadway at Bleecker St ☎ 982-8844 🚇 Broadway-Lafayette St 🚌 M21
⏰ Mon-Sat noon-7pm, Sun 1-6pm

Gianni Versace (2, J6)
Despite Gianni's tragic end at the hands of a murderer in 1997, his Italian high-fashion label lives on. Muster up attitude before you venture into the store.
✉ 815 Madison Ave at 68th St ☎ 744-6868
🚇 68th St 🚌 M1-4
⏰ Mon-Sat 10am-6pm

Giorgio Armani (2, K6) At this massive four-floor flagship store, you can browse in peace among gorgeous clothes, many of them unencumbered by the vulgarity of price tags.
✉ E 65th St at Madison Ave ☎ 988-9191
🚇 68th St, Lexington Ave (B, Q) 🚌 M1-4
⏰ Mon-Sat 10am-6pm (Thurs to 7pm)

Henry Lehr – T-Shirt (3, H6) Amid all of Nolita's delicate flouncery, it's good to see someone has an eye on the basics. This store is 90% T-shirts – cropped, long-sleeved, plain, striped, printed, embroidered – and they're all good quality.
✉ 268 Elizabeth St at Houston St ☎ 343-0567 🚇 Broadway-Lafayette St 🚌 M21
⏰ 11am-7pm

Jeffrey (3, E2)
High fashion in the Meatpacking District means runway pieces beside stylish knits and wacky

Secondhand Stores

While so many shoppers come to New York in search of that cutting-edge look, those with the retro urge will also find plenty of choices. On 7th St and St Marks Pl between 1st and 2nd Aves, a number of shops sell upscale secondhand stuff.

At **Screaming Mimi's** (382 Lafayette St at Great Jones St; 3, G6; ☎ 677-6464), the retro clothes and accessories include too-cool 1980s sunglasses, cotton shirts, bright dresses and anything synthetic. Choose among well-preserved vintage frocks and accessories from the 1930s to '60s at **The Stella Dallas Look** (218 Thompson St btw Bleecker & W 3rd St; 3, G5; ☎ 674-0447).

The secondhand clothing empire **Rags A Go Go** (73 E 7th St btw 1st & 2nd Aves; 3, F7; ☎ 254-4771) is good for not-too-expensive-but-never-crappy trend-chasing threads. The designer consignment store **Tokio 7** (64 E 7th St btw 1st & 2nd Aves; 3, F7; ☎ 353-8443) carries a sprinkling of top-name threads like Versace suits at around $200 or DKNY skirts for $20.

The cluttered **Village Scandal** (19 E 7th St btw 2nd & 3rd Aves; 3, F7; ☎ 460-9358) abounds with jewel-in-the-junk-heap dresses, shirts, suits and accessories that make you feel like dressing up every day.

reversible leatherwear. (But all come with go-figure price tags.) Uptown mothers and daughters fight over Prada flip-flops, while downtown dishes groove to the in-store DJ.

✉ **449 W 14th St btw 9th & 10th Aves** ☎ **206-3928** 🚇 **14th St-8th Ave** 🚌 **M14** 🕐 **Mon-Fri 10am-8pm (Thurs to 9pm), Sat 10am-7pm, Sun 12:30-6pm**

Wear out your shoes? Get a new pair at Pearl River.

Jill Anderson (3, F7)

One of the individualistic designers dotted along 9th St in the East Village, Anderson makes witty, retro-inflected clothes.

✉ **331 E 9th St btw 1st & 2nd Aves** ☎ **253-1747** 🚇 **1st Ave** 🚌 **M8** 🕐 **noon-8pm**

Nicole Miller (3, H5)

She's credited with reinventing the little black dress, but there's more to her repertoire than that. Expect well-made glam garb with kooky twists – a swish jacket with comic buttons, an evening gown held together with Velcro.

✉ **134 Prince St btw Wooster & W Broadway** ☎ **343-1362** 🚇 **Prince St, Broadway-Lafayette St** 🕐 **Mon-Sat 11am-7pm, Sun noon-6pm**

Pearl River (3, J6)

This Chinese supermarket sells everything from dollar novelties that fall apart as soon as you pay for them to carefully tended bonsai. You can also buy Chinese-style clothes in larger Western sizes.

✉ **277 Canal St at Broadway (also at 200 Grand St)** ☎ **431-4770** 🚇 **Canal St (J, M, N, R, Z, 6)** 🕐 **10am-7:30pm**

Polo/Ralph Lauren (2, H6)

Portraits of upper-crust youth and their ponies decorate this fragrant mansion. The clothes are crisp and understated, the customers handsome and recently shampooed.

✉ **Madison Ave at 72nd St** ☎ **606-2100** 🚇 **68th St** 🚌 **M1-4** 🕐 **Mon-Sat 10am-6pm**

Seize sur Vingt (3, H6)

To ensure your cuffs won't land in your soup, get your shirts made to measure here. Twenty measurements are taken for one Egyptian cotton shirt; stylish suits, pants, sweaters and boxers are also available.

✉ **243 Elizabeth St btw Houston & Prince Sts** ☎ **343-0476** 🚇 **Broadway-Lafayette St** 🕐 **Mon-Sat noon-7pm, Sun noon-6pm**

tg-170 (3, H8)

A variety of designers and styles mixes things up here. None of it seems designed to make you feel too fat or too old. Some of it, like Yinnub's reworkings of thrift store finds, might make you feel giggly.

✉ **170 Ludlow St at Stanton St** ☎ **995-8660** 🚇 **Delancey-Essex Sts** 🕐 **noon-8pm**

Tracy Feith (3, J6)

This large-for-its-location emporium specializes in urban-angel/country-sophisticate clothing – perfect for petite fashionelles with money to burn.

✉ **209 Mulberry St at Spring St** ☎ **334-3097** 🚇 **Spring St (6)** 🕐 **Mon-Sat 11am-7pm, Sun noon-7pm**

Vivienne Westwood (3, J5)

Always fun for a gander at the grandeur, punk's grand dame turns out a varied wardrobe of men's and women's wear. Some of the garments are sheer classic (though you'll still get a decent dose of loopy fashion).

✉ **71 Greene St btw Broome & Spring Sts** ☎ **334-5200** 🚇 **Spring St (6)** 🕐 **Mon-Sat 11am-7pm, Sun noon-6pm**

XLarge (3, H6)

Beastie Boy Mike D offers easywear for guys. Gals can fit into the X'Elle range. This is a good bet for cool – but not crazy – street clothes.

✉ **267 Lafayette St at Prince St** ☎ **334-4480** 🚇 **Prince St (N, R), Broadway-Lafayette St** 🕐 **noon-7pm**

ACCESSORIES

Amy Chan (3, H6)
You could base a whole outfit on these 'Where did you get your bag?' kind of bags. The wares include bum bags, tool belts, whimsical ballroom clutches and purses, all both pretty and practical.
✉ **247 Mulberry St btw Prince & Spring Sts**
☎ **966-3417**
🅱 Broadway-Lafayette St, Spring St (6), 2nd Ave 🚌 M21 ⏰ noon-7pm

Cartier (2, M6)
When the darlings of the diamond world first opened up shop in the US,

---

Not Too Taxing
New York's 8.25% sales tax has been waived on all clothing items under $110. This won't help out with your Armani wedding dress, but it makes minor apparel odysseys just that little bit easier.

---

they bought their 5th Ave site in exchange for a pearl necklace. Here you'll find rocks to knock your socks off and watches, glasses, bags and brooches all dying to become your new best friend.
✉ **653 5th Ave at 52nd St** ☎ **446-3460** 🅱 5th Ave (E, F) 🚌 M1-4 ⏰ Mon-Fri 10am-6pm, Sat 10am-5:30pm

Destinaton (3, F3)
Jacques Le Corre's trout-skin shoes and Serge Thoraval's romantic jewelry set a high bar for the artistic but functional merchandise here.
✉ **32-36 Little W 12th St btw Washington St & 9th Ave** ☎ **727-2031** 🅱 14th St-8th Ave 🚌 M14 ⏰ noon-8pm

Gruen Optika (2, K6)
This is the best store in the city for stand-out eyewear, whether you're looking for some funky shades or serious Wall St specs.
✉ **740 Madison Ave at 64th St** (call for other locations) ☎ **988-5832** 🅱 Lexington Ave (B, Q) 🚌 M1-4 ⏰ Mon-Fri 10am-6:30pm, Sat 10am-5pm, Sun noon-5pm

Otto Tootsi Plohound (3, D5)
Worship at the altar of tootsies – there's Prada and Miu Miu at the front, this season's copies at the rear and music banging all over.
✉ **137 5th Ave btw 19th & 20th Sts** (also at 413 W Broadway)
☎ **460-8650** 🅱 Union Sq ⏰ Mon-Fri 11:30am-7:30pm, Sat 11am-8pm, Sun noon-7pm

Tiffany & Co (2, L6)
It's not as snooty here as you might expect. If you look hard enough, you can take home a reasonably priced small item and get the impressive Tiffany's box.
✉ **727 5th Ave at 57th St** ☎ **755-8000** 🅱 57th St (B, Q), 5th Ave (N, R) 🚌 M1-4, M57 ⏰ Mon-Fri 10am-7pm, Sat 10am-6pm

ART & ANTIQUES

Antiquarium (2, H6)
If you've been eyeing an Egyptian sarcophagus at the Met, this is the place to buy one. The Egyptian and Near Eastern antiquities here include wearable antique jewelry and some modern pieces set with ancient coins.
✉ **948 Madison Ave at 75th St** ☎ **734-9776** 🅱 77th St 🚌 M1-4 ⏰ Tues-Sat 10am-5:30pm (shorter summer hrs)

Bernd Goeckler Antiques (3, F5)
Chandeliers and mirrors stand out among the inventory of Italian and French furniture from the 18th-century neoclassical period through art nouveau to art deco. When you're done, check out the other 10th St antique shops.
✉ **30 E 10th St at University Pl** ☎ **777-8209** 🅱 8th St-NYU 🚌 M8 ⏰ Mon-Fri 9am-6pm, Sat 10am-5pm

Bernhard & S Dean Levy (2, F6)
Owned by the same family for 100 years, this impeccable store contains five floors of American antiques from the 17th century to the early 19th century: paintings, silver, art, porcelain and sublime furniture.
✉ **24 E 84th St at Madison Ave** ☎ **628-7088** 🅱 86th St (4, 5, 6) 🚌 M1-4 ⏰ Tues-Sat 9:30am-5:30pm (Apr-Sept also open Mon)

Chelsea Antiques Building (3, C4)

Over several floors, more than 100 dealers offer the most concentrated selection of antiques in the city. The wares range from serious (18th-century mahogany tables) to fun (vintage cookie jars from the 1950s). The vast array of items draws hardcore collectors and haphazard browsers alike.

✉ 110 W 25th St btw 6th & 7th Aves ☎ 929-0909 Ⓜ 23rd St (F) 🚌 M23 ⏰ 10am-6pm

Dalva Brothers (2, L6)

This five-story showroom/townhouse would be worth a visit even if it didn't contain the country's biggest collection of European (particularly French) 18th-century furniture, porcelain, paintings and sculpture.

✉ 44 E 57th St btw Park & Madison Aves ☎ 758-2297 Ⓜ 5th Ave (N, E), 59th St (4, 5, 6) 🚌 M57 ⏰ Mon-Sat 10am-5:30pm (closed Sat in summer)

Going, Going, Gone

Frequent art and antique auctions happen in Manhattan, most of them free and open to the public. Check Friday's *New York Times* for listings or contact the houses directly: **Sotheby's** (1334 York Ave; 2, H9; ☎ 606-7010), **William Doyle Galleries** (175 E 87th St; 2, F7; ☎ 427-2730), **Tepper** (110 E 25th St at Park Ave S; 3, C6; ☎ 677-5300), **Christie's** (20 Rockefeller Plaza; 2, M6; ☎ 636-2000) and **Phillips** (3 W 57th St at 5th Ave; 2, L6; ☎ 570-4830).

Manhattan Art & Antiques Center

(2, L8) If you're not particularly focused and just want to see what's out there, come here; 100-plus different stores on three levels sell everything from Japanese curios to art deco Americana, from Chinese antiquities to French art glass.

✉ 1050 2nd Ave at 55th St ☎ 355-4400 📧 www.the-maac.com Ⓜ 59th St (4, 5, 6), Lexington Ave (N, R) 🚌 M57 ⏰ Mon-Sat 10:30am-6pm, Sun noon-6pm

Skyscraper (2, K8)

If furniture can say 'cocktail,' these American and European club chairs, dining settings and lamps are chattering. The art deco stock comes mostly from the 1930s and '40s, but some '50s stuff sneaks in, too. Among the accessories, the early digital clocks stand out.

✉ 237 E 60th St btw 2nd & 3rd Aves ☎ 588-0644 📧 www.skyscraperny.com Ⓜ 59th St (4, 5, 6), Lexington Ave (N, R) ⏰ Mon-Fri 10am-6pm, Sat 11am-5pm

Kim Grant

Signs of the times: antiques for sale on the Lower East Side

COMPUTERS & ELECTRONICS

New York (and, for foreign visitors, the US generally) is a good place to buy electronics, especially since the upsurge in sales over the Internet has forced retailers to keep prices down and extras (bonus gifts, extra service) up.

Bang & Olufson
(2, H6) Come here for the most expensive and best-designed electronic equipment in the world. If you don't want to outfit the whole lounge, consider the desk consoles, which are sublime, sexy and somewhat affordable.
✉ **952 Madison Ave at 75th St** ☎ **879-6161**
🚇 **77th St** 🚌 **M1-4**
🕐 **Mon-Sat 10am-6:30pm, Sun noon-5pm**

Window-shopping aplenty

Angus Oborn

B&H Photo (2, P4)
This huge camera store that carries new and used goods, digital and video gear prides itself on quality service and advice. Though there's pro equipment aplenty, the sales staff are happy to deal with amateur snappers.
✉ **420 9th Ave btw 33rd & 34th Sts**
☎ **444-6615** 🚇 **34th St-Penn Station (A, C, E)**
🚌 **M34** 🕐 **Mon-Thurs 9am-7pm, Fri 9am-1pm, Sun 10am-5pm**

J&R Music & Computer World
(3, M6) This massive store has a good reputation for selection and low prices on computers, videos, CDs and cameras, but the quality of the service varies. Avoid shopping on holiday weekends and at other busy times.
✉ **1-33 Park Row**
☎ **238-9100** 🚇 **City**

Hall 🕐 **Mon-Sat 9am-7pm (Thurs to 7:30pm), Sun 10:30am-6:30pm**

RCS (2, L6)
Browse among a decent selection of desktops, laptops, handhelds and software packages. The rushed staff are mostly well informed and helpful.
✉ **575 Madison Ave at 56th St** ☎ **949-6935**
🚇 **51st St (6), 5th Ave (E, F), 59th St (4, 5, 6)**
🕐 **Mon-Fri 9am-7pm, Sat 10am-6pm, Sun 11am-5pm**

Sony Style (2, L6)
Play with flashy new Sony products in the main showroom and be blown away by the home entertainment systems downstairs. Sony Wonder, on the premises, makes a great stop for kids (see p. 42).
✉ **550 Madison Ave at 56th St** ☎ **833-8000**
🚇 **51st St (6), 5th Ave (E, F), 59th St (4, 5, 6)**
🕐 **Mon-Sat 10am-7pm, Sun noon-6pm**

The Wiz (2, N6)
Nobody beats The Wiz – or so the commercials say. This discount chain sells electronics and appliances at good prices, but service varies. The many other stores in this chain include a large branch at 31st St & 6th Ave.
✉ **555 5th Ave at 46th St** ☎ **877-284-3949**
🚇 **Grand Central-42nd St** 🕐 **Mon-Sat 9am-8:30pm, Sun 11am-7pm**

Warning
Beware of smarmy, badgering and belligerent sales assistants in the discount electronics stores dotted around Times Square and along 5th Ave. If you buy, make sure you get a new, boxed product with documentation. If you feel ripped off, contact the Department of Consumer Affairs (☎ 487-4444; 🅴 www.ci.nyc.ny.us/consumers). Your rights include:

- a full refund within 20 days if the store has no other posted policy

- knowledge of the Manufacturer's Suggested Retail Price (stores must tell you the MSRP if they are charging above it)

MUSIC

New York is a good town to tune into the latest, greatest and spaciest and to hunt down personal classics that no one back home ever heard of. You'll find an array of offerings at big chains like Virgin Megastore (W 45th St at Broadway; 2, N5; ☎ 921-1020) and at small eclectic shops.

Academy Records & CDs (3, E5)

Music geeks flip through racks of classical, jazz, rock and pretty much whatever else you can think of, both new and used. A new East Village store (77 E 10th St) deals in LPs only.
✉ 12 W 18th St btw 5th & 6th Aves ☎ 242-3000 🚇 Union Sq, 23rd St ⏰ Mon-Sat 9:30am-9pm, Sun 11am-7pm

Bleecker Bob's (3, G4)

Here you'll find second-hand desirables and trash (mostly rock, R&B and folk) – stuff you've been looking for since you were 15 and stuff you never wanted to see again. You can buy rock T-shirts, too.
✉ 118 W 3rd St btw MacDougal St & 6th Ave ☎ 475-9677 🚇 W 4th St ⏰ 11am-1am (Fri-Sat to 3am)

Breakbeat Science (3, H7)

DJs flock to this store for platters of two-step garage, nu skool breaks, jungle and drum 'n' bass. The nice folks who run this host weekly parties – stop by the store and ask what's up.
✉ 181 Orchard St btw Houston & Stanton Sts ☎ 995-2592 🚇 2nd Ave (F) ⏰ 1-8pm (Thurs-Sat to 9pm)

Etherea (3, G8)

This small shop somehow manages to have every dance, electronic or indie CD or LP you're looking for. There's new and second-hand stock, often at snap-uppable prices.
✉ 66 Ave A at 5th St ☎ 358-1126 🚇 2nd Ave 🚌 M14 ⏰ noon-10pm (Fri-Sat to 11pm)

Footlight Records (3, F6)

Check out the magnificent collection of out-of-print albums, show music, Sinatra bootlegs and movie soundtracks on CD and LP.
✉ 113 E 12th St btw 3rd & 4th Aves ☎ 533-1572 🚇 Union Sq, 3rd Ave ⏰ Mon-Fri 11am-7pm, Sat 10am-6pm, Sun 11am-5pm

Other Music (3, G6)

This is the coolest store in town for electronic, experimental, indie and fusion, with a smattering of lounge, world and hip-hop – available new and used, on vinyl and CD.
✉ 15 E 4th St at Lafayette St ☎ 477-8150 🚇 Astor Pl ⏰ Mon-Sat noon-9pm (Fri to 10pm), Sun noon-7pm

Rocks in Your Head (3, H5)

The emphasis is on indie rock and imports, but there's also a decent selection of trance, hip-hop, art rock and blues among the new and used CDs and LPs.
✉ 157 Prince St btw W Broadway & Thompson St ☎ 475-6729 🚇 Prince St ⏰ noon-9pm (Fri-Sat to 10pm)

Tower Records (3, G6)

This huge chain store specializes in rock, pop and soul (classical, jazz and country are tucked away upstairs). For an equally vast selection of movies, stop at the massive Tower Books & Video store, one block east on Lafayette St.
✉ 692 Broadway at W 4th St ☎ 505-1500 🚇 Astor Pl ⏰ 9am-midnight

Rocks in Your Head: enough vinyl for ya?

Angus Oborn

BOOKS

Alabaster Bookshop

(3, E6) This small, select used bookstore offers a good range of fiction, art, photography and philosophy books, some of them rather rare.

✉ **122 4th Ave btw 12th & 13th Sts** ☎ **982-3550** Ⓜ **Union Sq** ⏲ **Mon-Thurs 10am-8pm, Fri-Sat 10am-10pm, Sun 11am-8pm**

Archivia (2, G6)

This lovely shop features beautiful used books on the decorative arts, architecture, gardening and interiors, many of them rare, out-of-print or otherwise hard to find.

✉ **2nd fl, 1063 Madison Ave at 80th St** ☎ **439-9194** Ⓜ **77th St** 🚌 **M1-4** ⏲ **Mon-Fri 10am-6pm, Sat-Sun noon-5pm**

The Argosy (2, L7)

Browse among estate-sale finds, rare prints, autographs, old maps, art books, classics and other eclectic used books on all topics. Bargain tables start at $1.

✉ **116 E 59th St btw**

Lexington & Park Aves

☎ **753-4455** Ⓜ **59th St (4, 5, 6), Lexington Ave (N, R)** ⏲ **Mon-Fri 10am-6pm (call for Sat hours)**

Barnes & Noble

(3, E5) Each of the many superstores features over 200,000 titles, comfortable seating and a café where you can read magazines and muse over potential purchases.

✉ **33 E 17th St at Union Sq** ☎ **253-0810** Ⓜ **Union Sq** ⏲ **10am-10pm**

Bluestockings (3, H7)

Read words for, by and about women in a comfy space that used to be a crack house. Performances or readings happen almost every evening.

✉ **172 Allen St at Stanton St** ☎ **777-6028** Ⓜ **2nd Ave** 🚌 **M15** ⏲ **Tues-Sat noon-8pm, Sun 2-8pm**

The Complete Traveller (3, B5)

Not only a handy place to pick up guides and maps for onward travel, this store is also a great spot to discover rare antiquarian travelogues and other far-flung and far-fetched esoterica.

✉ **199 Madison Ave at 35th St** ☎ **685-9007** Ⓜ **33rd St** ⏲ **Mon-Fri 9am-7pm, Sat 10am-6pm, Sun 11am-5pm**

Corner Bookstore

(2, D6) This small but select shop focuses on art books, fiction and children's literature. It's a comfortable place to browse and to listen to occasional author readings.

✉ **1313 Madison Ave at 93rd St** ☎ **831-3554** Ⓜ **96th St (6)** ⏲ **Mon-Thurs 10am-8pm, Fri 10am-7pm, Sat-Sun 11am-6pm**

Gotham Book Mart

(2, N6) One of the city's premier independent shops, this cluttered store that's been in business since 1920 is a real treasure. Its trademark shingle declares that 'wise men fish here'; WH Auden, Marianne Moore, Patti Smith and Woody Allen have all dangled a line.

✉ **41 W 47th St btw 5th & 6th Aves** ☎ **719-4448** Ⓜ **Rockefeller Center** ⏲ **Mon-Fri 9:30am-6:30pm, Sat 9:30am-6pm**

Housingworks Used Books Cafe (3, H6)

At this great airy space, you can read preloved books while enjoying coffee, pie, pasta or soup and basking in the knowledge that all profits go to benefit people with HIV and

---

Suggested Reading

You could spend the rest of your life reading books about New York – one is published every three days. Personal favorites include the stories of O Henry, warm and witty tales from the early 1900s; Paul Auster's *New York Trilogy*, spooky, Kafka-esque anti-spy stories; and Luc Sante's *Low Life*, a pithy history of poor and down-trodden 19th-century New Yorkers. EB White's 1949 essay *Here Is New York* is light, bright and absolutely right. For splashy, somewhat trashy tales of the modern city, pick up anything by Jay McInerney or Tama Janowitz. If you want an up-to-the-minute sense of the literary scene, grab *Open City*, a local literary journal.

AIDS. There are periodic readings and jazz sessions.

✉ **126 Crosby St btw Houston & Prince Sts**
☎ 334-3324
🚇 **Broadway-Lafayette St** 🚌 **M21** ⏰ **Mon-Wed 10am-8pm, Thurs-Fri 10am-9pm, Sat noon-9pm, Sun noon-7pm**

Jim Hanley's Universe (2, P6) Billing itself as a place 'where art and literature meet,' this comic book store carries the city's largest range of mainstream and independent titles, as well as toys, T-shirts and Jesus action figures.

✉ **4 W 33rd St at 5th Ave** ☎ 268-7088
🚇 **34th St-Herald Sq**
⏰ **Mon-Sat 9am-11pm, Sun 10am-9pm**

Printed Matter (3, D2) A stimulating nonprofit store dedicated to artists' publications, this shop offers 'book or book-like objects' produced in editions of 100 or more. The 'library' is a great place to browse through bent and beautiful offerings.

✉ **535 W 22nd St btw 10th & 11th Aves**
☎ 925-0325 🚇 **23rd St (C, E)** 🚌 **M23**
⏰ **Tues-Fri 10am-6pm, Sat 11am-7pm**

Rizzoli Bookstore (2, L6) It's hard not to swoon over the great art, architecture and design books in this beautiful store. The comfortable layout makes it easy to stroll from subject to subject and delightfully hard to leave.

✉ **31 W 57th St btw 5th & 6th Aves** ☎ 759-2424 🚇 **57th St (Q)**
⏰ **Mon-Sat 10am-7:30pm, Sun 11am-7pm**

Book browsing in New York: a full-time job

Angus Oborn

Shakespeare & Co (3, G6) The biggest of the four Shakespeare & Co stores in Manhattan, this pleasant shop carries a large selection of theater and film books and scripts. Downstairs you'll find more academic texts.

✉ **716 Broadway at Astor Pl (also at 939 Lexington Ave at 69th St, 1 Whitehall St, 137 E 23rd St at Lexington Ave)** ☎ 529-1330
🚇 **Astor Pl, 8th St**
⏰ **10am-11pm (Fri-Sat to midnight)**

St Marks Book Shop (3, F6) A lovely big bookshop with a neighborhood feel and an international outlook, St Marks has strong collections of political work, literature, poetry and academic journals.

✉ **31 3rd Ave at Stuyvesant St** ☎ 260-7853 🚇 **Astor Pl**
⏰ **Mon-Sat 10am-midnight, Sun 11am-mininight**

The Strand (3, F6) With 8 miles of used books and review copies, this landmark Manhattan bookstore is the kind of shop

that either inspires or crushes the aspiring writer. If you can't find enough here, visit the Strand Book Annex (Fulton & Gold Sts; 3, M6; ☎ 732-6070).

✉ **828 Broadway at 12th St** ☎ 473-1452
🚇 **Union Sq** ⏰ **Mon-Sat 9:30am-10:30pm, Sun 11am-10:30pm**

Traveler's Choice Bookstore (3, J5) Pick up guides, phrasebooks, dictionaries, language learning packs, maps, travel accessories – everything to inspire you to stay on the road.

✉ **2 Wooster St at Canal St** ☎ 941-1535
🚇 **Canal St (A, C, E)**
⏰ **Mon-Fri 9am-6pm**

Urban Center Books (2, M6) The Municipal Arts Society runs this beautiful bookstore, specializing in architecture and design, inside the ornate Villard Apartments. Adjacent exhibition spaces house design-related shows.

✉ **457 Madison Ave at 51st St** ☎ 935-3595
🚇 **51st St** ⏰ **Sun-Thurs 10am-7pm, Fri 10am-6pm, Sat 10am-5:30pm**

FOOD & DRINK

If you're making your own meals or just picnicking, a plethora of food stores offer a wonderful range of goodies. And because this is New York, and we're all very busy, just about all of these stores will make you a meal to eat on the run.

Balducci (3, F4)
In the right season, choose from a dozen sorts of tomatoes, lose yourself in 'mushroom corner' or swoon before the cheese display.
✉ 6th Ave at 9th St
☎ 673-2600 🚇 6th Ave ⏰ 7am-8:30pm

Butterfield Market (2, G7) What this long-standing house of delectables lacks in size it makes up for in well-selected necessities, gourmet treats and informed staff. Kitchenware includes a very cute selection of bird-shaped teapots.
✉ 1114 Lexington Ave at 78th St ☎ 288-7500 🚇 77th St 🚌 M101-103 ⏰ Mon-Fri 7:30am-8pm, Sat 7:30am-5:30pm, Sun 8am-5pm

Chelsea Market (3, E3)
At this big food complex in an old cookie factory, the on-view cooking makes shopping for bread, soup, cheese, wine, kitchen supplies and flowers more fun.
✉ 75 9th Ave btw 15th & 16th Sts ☎ 243-6005 🚇 14th St-8th Ave 🚌 M14 ⏰ Mon-Sat 8am-7pm, Sun 10am-6pm

Dowel Quality Products (3, G7)
This Indian grocery is worth ducking into just to soak up the smell: take a wonderful whiff of the spices, lentils, rice and curry. The small selection of fresh vegetables and meat leaves room for 400 varieties of beer.
✉ 91 1st Ave at 6th St ☎ 979-6045 🚇 1st Ave 🚌 M15 ⏰ 11am-1am

Economy Candy (3, H8) This big discount candy store sells chocolates, halva, nuts, coffee and dried fruit from around the world – stop in to soothe your inner zit.
✉ 108 Rivington St btw Essex & Ludlow Sts ☎ 254-1531 🚇 Delancey-Essex Sts 🚌 M9, M14 ⏰ Sun-Fri 9am-6pm, Sat 10am-5pm

Sherry-Lehman (2, K6)
This world-class wine and spirits store, in business for six decades, features reasonable prices and knowledgeable staff who can help you pick the right wine for the occasion.
✉ 679 Madison Ave at 61st St ☎ 838-7500 🚇 5th Ave (N, R) ⏰ Mon-Sat 9am-7pm

Vintage New York (3, J5) New York State has about 140 wineries, but you'd never know it by looking in most local wine stores. At this shop, you can taste and buy local varieties like Seyval Blanc, Vignoles and Vidal, plus cheese, chocolate and deli goodies to bulk up your hamper.
✉ 482 Broome St at Wooster St ☎ 226-9463 🚇 Canal St (A, C, E) ⏰ Mon-Sat 11am-9pm, Sun noon-9pm

Zabar's (2, G3)
The city's most popular gourmet food emporium is cluttered in just the right way – it's a feast of sights and smells, both packaged and fresh. Try the great selection of house-made soups. An attached cafeteria serves drinks and pastries. For espresso machines and other kitchenware, head upstairs.
✉ Broadway at 80th St ☎ 787-2000 🚇 79th St ⏰ Mon-Fri 8am-7:30pm, Sat 8am-8pm, Sun 9am-6pm

Abundance of edibles: Zabar's

FOR CHILDREN

Plenty of Big Apple businesses keep junior shoppers entertained. Crowds gravitate to the ever-popular Disney Store (711 5th Ave at 55th St; 2, L6; ☎ 702-0702) and Warner Bros Studio Store (1 Times Sq; 2, N5; ☎ 840-4040), but New York also boasts more unique kid stuff.

Drawing up Santa's shopping list at the Disney Store

Books of Wonder
(3, E5) This store abounds with children's titles and young adult fiction both new and old, rare and collectible. Author readings take place most weekends.
✉ 16 W 18th St btw 5th & 6th Aves ☎ 989-3270 🚇 Union Sq
🕐 Mon-Sat 10am-7pm, Sun noon-6pm

The Enchanted Forest
(3, H5) There's hardly anything that needs batteries at this delightful store with wonderful books, teddy bears, hand puppets and games – many made to please more than to teach.
✉ 85 Mercer St at Spring St ☎ 925-6677 🚇 Spring St (6)
🕐 Mon-Sat 11am-7pm, Sun noon-6pm

FAO Schwarz (2, L6)
The most crowded, expensive and elaborate toy store in town includes a wildly popular Barbie salon. A 'schweetz' store promises to keep the kids hyper.
✉ 767 5th Ave at 58th St ☎ 644-9400 🚇 5th Ave (N, R)

🕐 Mon-Wed 10am-6pm, Thurs-Sat 10am-8pm, Sun 11am-7pm

Gymboree (2, F6)
This big chain sells colorful, durable, reasonably priced casual clothing for newborns to seven-year-olds. Good materials, smartly manufactured, make for easy mix-and-matching.
✉ 1120 Madison Ave at 83rd St (call for other locations)
☎ 717-6702 🚇 86th St (4, 5, 6) 🕐 Mon-Fri 10am-7pm, Sat 10am-6pm, Sun noon-5pm

Tot toys: FAO Schwarz

Infinity (2, F6)
This rumble-tumble store features piles, racks and packed nooks of clothing for boys and girls, whether you're looking for playground duds, school sweaters or small-size formal wear.
✉ 1116 Madison Ave at 83rd St ☎ 517-4232 🚇 86th St (4, 5, 6)
🕐 10am-6pm

Little Eric (2, F6)
Shoes for little feet walk (no running!) out of this well-stocked store with a kid-friendly staff. Eric's got boots to suit everyone from little men to homeboys, baby ballerinas to party dolls. The gumboots (galoshes) are the most super sloshers around.
✉ 1118 Madison Ave at 83rd St (also at 1331 3rd Ave at 76th St)
☎ 717-1513 🚇 86th St (4, 5, 6) 🕐 Mon-Sat 10am-6pm, Sun noon-5pm

Zittles (2, H6)
This cluttered find offers all the old toy-store faves – costumes, masks, jigsaws – and a smart selection of silicon-chip toys with an educational bent. The pet emporium next door (No 965) features a bakery for dogs.
✉ 3rd fl, 969 Madison Ave at 75th St ☎ 644-9400 🚇 77th St
🕐 Mon-Fri 9am-8pm, Sat 9am-7pm, Sun 10am-6pm

SPECIALTY ITEMS

Davidoff of Geneva

(2, M6) Big men in rumpled suits stroll in here to shop for cologne, ties, ashtrays, cigars, pipes and tobacco – in fact, everything smokable except Cuban cigars.
✉ Madison Ave at 54th St ☎ 751-9060 🚇 5th Ave (E, F) ⏰ Mon-Fri 10am-6:30pm, Sat 10am-6pm

Dö Kham (3, H6)

This store is best known for its gorgeous Tibetan fur-trimmed hats, but it's also full of exquisite gifts and wearables, many of the wares made by Tibetan refugees.
✉ 51 Prince St at Mulberry St ☎ 966-2404 🚇 Prince St ⏰ 10am-8pm

Flight 001 (3, E3)

Definitely the coolest shop in town for travel products, Flight 001 loves the small stuff. Choose among well-designed bags, gadgets, bits and bobs before you set off on your journey home.
✉ 96 Greenwich Ave at 12th St ☎ 691-1001 🚇 14th St-8th Ave ⏰ Mon-Fri 11am-8:30pm, Sat 11am-8pm, Sun noon-6pm

Flynn's School of Herbology (3, G6)

At this tiny, fragrant 'medicine shop,' you'll find herbs, potions, oils and lotions. Colon therapy is also available (yikes!).
✉ 60 E 4th St at Bowery ☎ 677-8140 🚇 Bleecker St ⏰ Fri-Sat noon-7pm

Hammacher Schlemmer (2, L7)

Get out your wallets for amazing, kooky gadgets, gizmos and gifts. Everything, from the microwave flower press to the massage seat with sound system, has been rigorously tested.
✉ 147 E 57th St btw Lexington & 3rd Aves ☎ 421-9000 🚇 Lexington Ave (N, R), 59th St (4, 5, 6) ⏰ Mon-Sat 10am-6pm

Kiehl's (3, E6)

This quirky pharmacy has been selling delicious organic skin-care products since 1851. Loyal customers include admirers of the late owner's Harley-Davidson collection.
✉ 109 3rd Ave at 13th St ☎ 475-3400 🚇 3rd Ave ⏰ Mon-Fri 10am-6:30pm (Thurs to 7:30pm), Sat 10am-6pm

Mackenzie-Childs

(2, J6) This overwhelming store is absolutely packed with country-cottage housewares and furniture. Don't miss the miniature mansion on the top level.
✉ 824 Madison Ave at 69th St ☎ 570-6050 🚇 68th St ⏰ Mon-Sat 10am-6pm

MoMA Design Store

(2, M6) Watches, kitchenware, toys, scarves, chairs, desk tidies: if it's in this store, it's beautiful. Come here to find great gifts.
✉ 44 W 53rd St btw 5th & 6th Aves ☎ 767-1050 🚇 5th Ave (E, F) ⏰ 10am-6:30pm (Fri to 8pm)

Paragon Athletic Goods (3, D5)

Mayhem breaks out on weekends, as New Yorkers snap up inline skates, scooters and other sports gear for some active R&R. The prices here regularly beat those of the chain stores.
✉ 867 Broadway at 18th St ☎ 255-8036 🚇 Union Sq ⏰ Mon-Sat 10am-8pm, Sun 11am-6:30pm

Toys in Babeland

(3, H8) Men and women are both welcome at this sweet-smelling, unsleazy sex shop that sells toys, videos and books (including a vagina coloring book). You can also stop in for a sex-celebratory workshop (eg, 'Fill 'Er Up – Fisting Basics').
✉ 94 Rivington St at Ludlow St ☎ 375-1701 🚇 Delancey-Essex Sts ⏰ Tues-Sat noon-10pm, Sun noon-8pm

Flight 001 gets you ready for takeoff.

places to eat

If you're hungry in New York, you're just not trying – it's a fabulous town for food. With around 20,000 places to eat spread through the city, the

Meals on wheels

possibilities are effectively endless: you could have dinner at a different restaurant every night for 50 years, running the gourmet gamut from hot dog to top-notch noshery and back again.

New York Cuisine

The immigrant nature of New York is expressed nowhere better than in its food. You can eat by neighborhood – Chinese in Chinatown, Italian in Little Italy – or wander a little wider and wilder. Not only are there restaurants serving just about every ethnic cuisine imaginable, but the melting pot has moved beyond Tex-Mex to such unlikely sounding cultural fusions as Cuban-Chinese and Indian-French. It seems to be only French restaurants that make it hard to eat vegetarian; most New York eateries are conscious of the need to offer herbivorous meals – see p. 71 for vegetarian recommendations.

Drinks

Keep an eye on your alcohol intake, as restaurants savagely mark up drinks. If you want to sip sedately, house wine by the glass is usually pretty good. If you ask for water, specify that you want tap water unless you're happy to quaff expensive bottled H_2O.

Tipping & Tax

The standard tip for meals is 15-20%; double the 8% sales tax listed on your bill, and you'll be leaving a reasonable gratuity. Many places add a 'service charge' for groups of six or more – you're not required to tip extra. In casual eateries where you order your meal at the counter, tipping is optional.

Reservations

To avoid waiting in line or being turned away at the door, make reservations for any restaurants above diner level. Reservations are often essential on weekends.

Opening Hours

Most eateries are open daily, but if they take a day off, it's likely to be Monday. Specific restaurant opening hours are provided with reviews in this chapter.

How Much?

The symbols used in this chapter indicate the cost of a main course, without drinks, tax or tips.

$	under $10
$$	$10-19
$$$	$20-29
$$$$	$30+

Look out for prix fixe offers.

Angus Oborn

Breakfast & Brunch

New Yorkers never seem to eat breakfast at home, preferring to head out to one of the city's hundreds of cafés and diners for cooked breakfasts, bagels or 'cawfee' on the run.

It's bizarre that people as impatient as New Yorkers don't mind lining up for weekend brunch (almost always eaten over a copy of the *New York Times*). Most cafés and a good number of restaurants prepare special brunch offerings, served from 11am to 4pm-ish. The classics are eggs, waffles, pancakes and French toast, but most places also offer cereals, fruit and pastries. Bloody Marys and mimosas are standard brunch beverages – you'd be surprised how smoothly they go down with fried fare.

New York's picks of the brunch crop include **Sarabeth's** (p. 82), **The Grange Hall** (p. 74), **EJ's Luncheonette** (p. 83), **Diner** (p. 69) and **Odessa** (see 'Eating around the Clock').

Eating around the Clock

The best 24-hour options include:

Bereket (187 E Houston St at Orchard St; 3, H7; ☎ 475-7700; $) – Turkish kebabs and good vegetarian falafel

Empire (210 10th Ave at 22nd St; 3, D2; ☎ 243-2736; $) – chrome boxcar diner where celebrities go for fries

French Roast (78 W 11th St at 6th Ave; 3, F4; ☎ 533-2233; $$) – salads, sandwiches, desserts in a casual atmosphere

Odessa (119 Ave A at E 7th St; 3, F8; ☎ 253-1470; $) – French toast with challah bread, blintzes and pierogies

Also try **Veselka** (p. 72), **Florent** (p. 74) and **Kangsuh Korean Restaurant** (p. 79).

Mulling over the menu at Veselka

Angus Oborn

Lunch

Generally, lunch is served from 11am to 2:30pm. Midtown restaurants may not serve lunch on weekends, while Lower Manhattan restaurants often close altogether over the weekend. See 'Taking Care of Business' (p. 78) for some of the best spots for a business lunch.

Dinner & Beyond

Restaurants usually serve the evening meal between 5 and 10pm, though most kitchens stay in business later on Friday and Saturday. But when dawn's on its way and you're clubbed out, there's no need to go hungry. New York understands how a midnight snack can suddenly seem as distant as yesterday's breakfast (see 'Eating around the Clock').

Restaurant Weeks

New York has two 'restaurant weeks,' one in January and one in late June, when 150 of the city's better restaurants offer prix fixe lunches for a smidge over $20. Increasingly, more restaurants are extending the deals throughout the year. Check out **e** www.restaurantweek.com or ask at the tourist office.

BROOKLYN

Blue Ribbon

(6, G2)   **$$$**

Modern American

The Sullivan St (Soho) late-night foodie hangout of the same name has spawned a sister on the Slope. And from the word go, the huge buzz has drawn crowds. Get eating because it's too noisy to chat: start with oysters, ribs or pierogies and move onto crabs, lobster, paella or tricked-up classics.

✉ **280 5th Ave at 1st St, Park Slope** ☎ **718-840-0404** Ⓢ **Union St** 🚍 **B63** ⏱ **Tues-Sun 6pm-4am**

Caffe Volna (6, K4) **$$**

Russian

Along the boardwalk, a 15-minute stroll from Coney Island, this is one of a string of Russian cafés serving blintzes, herring, kebabs, stroganoff, sturgeon and borscht. Just like a real Russian restaurant, it may or may not have what you ask for, and if it does, staff may or may not serve you with a smile.

✉ **3145 Brighton 4th St, Brighton Beach** ☎ **718-332-0501** Ⓢ **Aquarium** 🚍 **B1, B68** ⏱ **9am-11pm** ♿

Diner (6, F2)   **$$**

American

This hipster boxcar diner thrives in a nowhere zone under the Williamsburg Bridge. Don't fret about the minimal burger-and-steak menu – seasonal specials are creative and excellent. A recent version of the always-good vegetable plate included grilled asparagus, red onion and marinated capsicum on bulgur.

✉ **85 Broadway at S 7th St, Williamsburg** ☎ **718-486-3077** Ⓢ **Marcy Ave** ⏱ **11am-midnight (Fri-Sat to 1am)** Ⓥ

Henry's End (3, N9) **$$**

Modern American

Walk over the Brooklyn Bridge to this pleasant bistro with a fine eye for matching mostly American wines (by the bottle or glass) with mostly meaty foods. The duckling – boned, crisped and braised – is a specialty, but it's all creative and tantalizing. Reservations recommended for three or more.

✉ **44 Henry St btw Middagh & Cranberry Sts, Brooklyn Heights** ☎ **718-834-1776** Ⓢ **Clark St** ⏱ **Mon-Sat 5:30-10:30pm (Fri-Sat to 11:30pm), Sun 5-10pm**

Plan-Eat Thailand

(6, E2)   **$$**

Thai-Japanese

This massive Asian food theme park boasts a good Thai menu (noodles and seafood with ginger, coconut and chili accents), plus a hibachi grill and sushi bar. The food is tasty, and, despite the scale of the hubbub, service is brisk. Expect a long wait on weekends, when the Manhattanites stream in.

✉ **141 N 7th St btw Bedford Ave & Berry St, Williamsburg** ☎ **718-599-5758** Ⓢ **Bedford Ave (L)** 🚍 **B39, B61** ⏱ **11:30am-1am (Thurs-Sat to 2am)** ♿ Ⓥ

CHELSEA/UNION SQUARE

Commune (3, D5) **$$$**

American

'Eat, drink and be merry' is the order on the awning, and the patrons don't have trouble complying. Come for a drink or brash, hearty plates of American nosh.

✉ **12 E 22nd St at 5th Ave** ☎ **777-2600** Ⓢ **23rd St (N, R)** ⏱ **Mon noon-11pm, Tues-Fri noon-1am, Sat 11am-1am, Sun 11am-11pm**

The Dish (3, D3)   **$**

American

This unpretentious modern diner serves gourmet sandwiches, great shakes, lots of pasta and classic breakfasts. Sit and read the paper on weekdays; weekends, see who's pulled up how from the night before.

✉ **201 8th Ave at 20th St** ☎ **352-9800** Ⓢ **23rd St (C, E)** ⏱ **7am-midnight (Fri-Sat to 2am)** ♿ Ⓥ

El Cid (3, E3)   **$$**

Spanish

Tight-knit tables and a long bar fill this smallish but rollicking tapas place with lines out the door. Consider your choices over a pitcher of sangria – the grilled sardines make a good pick, as do the chorizo al vino and the pork cutlets. Reservations recommended.

✉ **322 W 15th St btw 8th & 9th Aves** ☎ **929-9332** Ⓢ **8th Ave**

⊟ M14 ⏱ lunch Tues-Fri noon-3pm, dinner Tues-Sun 5-11pm (Fri-Sat to 11:30pm) ♿

Le Gamin (3, D3) $
French Café
Pencil on a moustache, say 'mais oui' with an arch smile and get to Gamin ('urchin,' in French) for café au lait, crêpes and air kisses. This branch features lazy ceiling fans, pressed-tin walls and a parade of composed and attractive customers (including your good self).
✉ 183 9th Ave at W 21st St (also at 50 MacDougal St; Les Deux Gamins, 170 Waverly Pl) ☎ 243-8864 🚇 23rd St (C, E) ⊟ M23 ⏱ 8am-midnight ♿ V

Sushi Samba (3, D6) $$$
Peruvian-Japanese
Mixing Japanese and Peruvian cuisine might seem strange, but when you think sushi and ceviches (citrus-marinated seafood), the puzzle fits together like mackerel and blood orange. Add a pinch of Brazilian Carnivale and you've got this glitzy, popular concept restaurant, which also serves meat skewers and vegetarian dishes, as well as its signature seafood.
✉ 245 Park Ave S btw 19th & 20th Sts (also at 7th Ave & Barrow St) ☎ 475-9377 🚇 23rd St (6) ⏱ Mon-Wed noon-1am, Thurs-Sat noon-2am, Sun noon-midnight V

Roll with a Hole

Bagels are as New York as yellow cabs and subway evangelists. The classic hand-rolled, boiled bagel is bald and shiny, but they also come studded with sesame and poppy seeds, onion and garlic bits, or all of the above (try the 'everything' variety). Various vegetable and smoked fish 'shmears' (cream cheese spreads) make popular toppings. Our favorite bagelries include:

Barney Greengrass (541 Amsterdam Ave at 86th St; 2, F3) – amazing smoked-salmon bagels

Ess-a-Bagel (831 3rd Ave btw 50th & 51st Sts; 2, M7; also at 359 1st Ave) – classic Jewish bagels

H&H Bagels (2239 Broadway at 80th St; 2, G3) – sugary, addictive bagels

Murray's (500 6th Ave btw 12th & 13th Sts; 3, E4) – sun-dried tomato bagels and other gourmet versions

Angus Oborn

Zen Palate, alfresco

Union Square Coffee Shop (3, E5) $$
American-Brazilian
Brazilian specials like Moqueca Stew (with seafood) add some color to the New American menu at this trendy restaurant/bar. The always-high noise level rises to cacophonic at busy times. The reliably gorgeous waiting staff (cross dressers late at night) provide just about adequate service. Reservations recommended Thursday to Sunday.
✉ 29 Union Sq W at 16th St ☎ 243-7969 🚇 Union Sq ⏱ Mon 7am-2am, Tues 7am-4am, Wed-Fri 7am-5:30am, Sat 8am-5:30am, Sun 8am-2am V

Zen Palate (3, E6) $$
Vegetarian
The multicultural vegetarian food tends to favor Asian cuisine, but pasta, mashed potatoes and 'vegiloaf' make it onto the menu. Downstairs is casual; upstairs is more formal. Reservations recommended upstairs.
✉ 34 E Union Sq at 16th St ☎ 614-9345 🚇 Union Sq ⏱ Mon-Fri 11:30am-10:30pm, Sat 11:30am-midnight, Sun noon-10pm ♿ V

CHINATOWN

Great New York Noodle Town (3, K7) $
Chinese
The crowd in this always-busy restaurant includes old Chinese couples slurping soupy noodles and worshippers of the salt-baked softshell crab (when in season). It's not salubrious – the carcasses in the kitchen are in full view – but you can't beat the price and taste.
✉ 28½ Bowery at Bayard St ☎ 349-0923 🚇 Canal St (J, M, N, R, Z, 6) ⏰ 9am-4am ⚕ V

Marco Polo Noodle Shop (3, K6) $
Chinese
Forget about the lines at the nearby restaurants and turn to this cheap, bright spot where the cooks make their own lovely noodles (you can see them being churned out on the hand-driven pasta machine in the kitchen).
✉ 94 Baxter St at Canal St ☎ 941-6679 🚇 Canal St (N, R, S, 6, J, M, Z) ⏰ 11am-11pm ⚕ V

Pho Bang (3, J6) $
Vietnamese
For soup with a fragrant bang (never a whimper), try this clean and spacious restaurant. The spicy and sour fish soup (with salmon, okra and pineapple) is a fortifying favorite with jurors from the courts nearby.
✉ 157 Mott St btw Grand & Broome Sts ☎ 966-3797 🚇 Bowery ⏰ 10am-10pm ⚕ V

Pho Viet Huong (3, K6) $
Vietnamese
The smell of fresh herbs hits you as you walk into this large restaurant with a dinky bamboo courtyard theme and an overwhelmingly varied menu. The clay-pot curries and fondues arrive burbling, and the vegetables are crisp and glistening (but not at all greasy). Try the great soups.
✉ 73 Mulberry St at Bayard St ☎ 233-8988 🚇 Canal St (J, M, N, R, Z, 6) ⏰ 10:30am-10:30pm ⚕ V

Saint's Alp Teahouse (3, K7) $
Taiwanese
This Taiwanese-style teahouse serves green tea and a selection of frothy iced teas with tapioca balls (they come with a fat straw so you can suck up the spheres). Snacks include hotcakes with coconut butter and cuttlefish balls.
✉ 51 Mott St btw Bayard & Pell Sts ☎ 766-9889 🚇 Canal St (N, R, S, 6, J, M, Z) ⏰ Sun-Thurs 11am-11:30pm, Fri-Sat 11:30am-midnight ⚕ V

Do-it-yourself meals in Chinatown

Flesh-Free & Fabulous
New York City makes for relatively easy vegetarian eating, but a few standout places have devoted themselves to the herbivore cause. **The Herban Kitchen** (290 Hudson St at Spring St; 3, J4; ☎ 627-2257; $$) gets creative with organic fare. **The Sanctuary** (25 1st Ave btw 1st & 2nd Sts; 3, G7; ☎ 780-9786; $$) is the place to chow on karma-free fakin' bacon. Chinatown options include the **House of Vegetarian** (68 Mott St at Bayard St; 3, K7; ☎ 226-6572; $) and **Vegetarian Paradise 3** (33 Mott St at Pell St; 3, K7; ☎ 406-6988; $). **Spring Street Natural** (p. 80) and **Zen Palate** (p. 70) also do a good job with meat-free meals.

EAST VILLAGE

Angelica Kitchen (3, F7) $
Vegan
This remnant from the hippie era serves 95% organic, 100% vegan food to a fiber-rich crowd in a glossy pine setting. The picnic plates make great lunches if you're having a high-energy day. The communal table is a comfortable – and potentially chatty – place to eat alone.
✉ 300 E 12th St btw 1st & 2nd Aves ☎ 228-2909 Ⓜ 1st Ave ⏰ 11:30am-10:30pm ♿ Ⓥ

Cafe Mogador (3, F7) $
Moroccan
Duck out of the main St Marks drag and try some excellent couscous, merguez (spicy beef sausage) and harissa (hot sauce). This makes a good spot to split dips with a buddy or to eat a solo sandwich with the newspaper. Weekend nights it heats up with music and lots of chatter.
✉ 101 St Marks Pl btw Ave A & 1st Ave ☎ 677-2226 Ⓜ 1st Ave Ⓜ M14 ⏰ 9am-12:30am (Fri-Sat to 1:30am) ♿ Ⓥ

Dok Suni (3, F7) $$
Korean
Eat early to beat the crowds who come to eat delicious Korean home cookin' at this small and deservedly popular restaurant. Try the good vegetable dumplings or moochim (warm salad in red-pepper sauce) with squid, beef or veggies.
✉ 119 1st Ave btw 7th St & St Marks Pl ☎ 477-9506 Ⓜ 1st Ave Ⓜ M15 ⏰ Sun-Mon 4:30pm-11pm, Tues-Sat 4:30pm-midnight Ⓥ

Kimchi, anyone?

Hasaki (3, F6) $$
Japanese
Dotted with good sushi restaurants, E 9th St is something of a Little Tokyo. Hasaki has the best reputation, so head there first but if there's a long wait, go next door to Sharaku.
✉ 210 E 9th St btw 2nd & 3rd Aves ☎ 473-3327 Ⓜ Astor Pl ⏰ 5:30-11:30pm (also Sat-Sun 1-4pm)

La Paella (3, F6) $$
Spanish
This lively tavern offers good tapas, sangria and, of course, paella. The big daddy Español comes with the whole barnyard and aquarium: chorizo, chicken, clams, mussels, squid and prawns. Low-talkers and long-legged folk: get ready for noise and tight quarters.
✉ 214 E 9th St btw 2nd & 3rd Aves ☎ 598-4321 Ⓜ Astor Pl ⏰ 5-10:30pm ♿ Ⓥ

La Palapa (3, G8) $$
Mexican
This modern, stylish cocina has caused a stir with regional Mexican dishes like grilled cactus leaf, chili-rubbed chicken taco and cinnamon empanada.

Jewish Delis

The East Village is the place to get skyscraper-size sandwiches and kissable knishes. **Katz's** (205 E Houston St at Ludlow St; 3, H8; $) has been serving up pastrami on rye since 1888. The **Second Ave Deli** (156 2nd Ave at E 10th St; 3, F7; $) does a mean matzo-ball soup. **Veselka** (144 2nd Ave at E 9th St; 3, F7; $) makes brilliant borsht and perfect piroshkis and pancakes. **Yonah Shimmel Knish Bakery** (137 E Houston St btw 1st & 2nd Aves; 3, H7; $) offers sweet and savory knishes, latkes and blintzes.

They're all a pretty good value for your buck.
✉ 77 St Mark's Pl btw 1st & 2nd Aves ☎ 777-2537 🚇 Astor Pl ◷ Mon-Sat noon-midnight, Sat-Sun 11am-midnight V

Mama's (3, G8) $
Southern
This is where the East Village goes for eat-yo-greens fare. Point and get plated: fried, grilled or roasted chicken, grilled fish and more than a dozen luscious all-vegetarian sides (the soggy sweet potato in honey glaze is stupendous). Mama says, 'Shut up and eat it!'
✉ 200 E 3rd St btw Aves A & B ☎ 777-4425 🚇 2nd Ave 🚌 M14, M21 ◷ Mon-Sat noon-10pm ♿ V

Panna II (3, G7) $
Indian
The interior must be seen to be believed: the profusion of lights, glitter and baubles hanging from the ceiling means that the waiters serve the food hunched double. Even though the curries and tandoori dishes are only okay, it's hard not to have a good time here. Bring Indian beer from Dowel, next door.
✉ 93 1st Ave btw 5th & 6th Sts ☎ 598-4610 🚇 2nd Ave 🚌 M15 ◷ noon-11:30pm ♿ V

Prune (3, G7) $$
Modern American
This jaunty restaurant takes a fresh look at hearty home-style food, with dishes like pork poached in milk and cod in olive oil and good bar snacks, too. It's very New East Village –

Have a seat and make yourself at home at Mama's.

tiny, busy and loud.
✉ 54 E 1st St btw 1st & 2nd Aves ☎ 677-6221 🚇 2nd Ave ◷ Mon-Sat 6-11pm (Fri-Sat to midnight), Sun 5-10pm

Raga (3, G7) $$
Indian
With 'Indian-inspired cuisine' that hits the spot, Raga offers tandoori steak and swordfish over basmati rice in a stylin' but friendly setting with a neighborhood feel. A nice wine list complements the meals. Early evening prix fixe meals are available. Reservations recommended Friday and Saturday.
✉ 433 E 6th St btw Ave A & 1st Ave ☎ 388-0957 🚇 1st Ave 🚌 M14 ◷ 6-11pm (Fri-Sun to midnight); call for weekend brunch hrs ♿ V

Tappo (3, F7) $$$
Mediterranean
Large for the area, this newish place reels in

crowds with dishes like grilled baby octopus with tabouli and roasted rabbit with sage leaves. A large part of the menu changes daily; the appetizers are always good for sharing.
✉ 403 E 12th St at 1st Ave ☎ 505-0001 🚇 1st Ave ◷ lunch Fri-Sun noon-4pm; dinner Mon-Sat 6pm-midnight (Fri-Sat to 1am), Sun 5pm-midnight

Veniero's (3, F7) $
Bakery
This cake shop and bakery has been sugaring up the East Village for more than a century. Take a number and wait at the counter or line up to sit down in the glowing dining room. The cheesecakes are sensational, and the miniature eclairs, custard tarts and biscotti make great gifts or instant scoff fodder.
✉ 342 E 11th St at 1st Ave ☎ 674-7070 🚇 1st Ave ◷ 8am-11:45pm (Fri-Sat to 1am) ♿ V

GREENWICH VILLAGE/WEST VILLAGE

Cornelia Street Cafe (3, G4) $$

Modern American
Expect great food, accommodating service and entertainment every night, including readings and mostly jazzy music. On the menu? Perky modern meals like lemon asparagus risotto and sesame-crusted salmon. Brunch is big. Reservations recommended on weekends.
✉ 29 Cornelia St at Bleecker St ☎ 989-9319 🚇 W 4th St
🕐 10am-1am (Fri-Sat to 1:30am) ♿ [V]

Corner Bistro (3, F3) $

Burgers
Our notes about this legendary burger bar are slurred, sloppy and stained. We quote: 'forhet about yr met eating compainions – m burgwr whichn is ruined just yby putting it down a majoir burger fauxb oas.' Summation: come here late at night when you're drunk. It's great.
✉ 331 W 4th St at Jane St ☎ 242-9502
🚇 14th St-8th Ave
🚌 M14 🕐 11:30am-4am

Florent (3, F2) $$

French-American
This Meatpacking District pioneer keeps hauling 'em in because it's just great! Pre-, post- or 'tween club, the modish diner makes a great stop for boudin noir (blood sausage), pork chops and mussels – all justly lauded. The breakfasts make for a good start to the day. For dessert, try the cakes. Reservations recommended. Cash only.
✉ 69 Gansevoort St btw Greenwich & Washington Sts
☎ 989-5779 🚇 14th St-8th Ave 🚌 M14
🕐 Mon-Thurs 9am-5am, Fri-Sun 24hrs [V]

The Grange Hall (3, G4) $$

Classic American
A big harvest mural sets the tone at this airy, restored speakeasy with a renowned weekend brunch. The hearty main dishes (mostly roasted, baked or grilled meats) come 'simple' (with vegetable or salad accompaniment) or 'complete' (with soup or salad, as well).

Reservations recommended for dinner Thursday to Saturday and for brunch.
✉ 50 Commerce St at Bedford St ☎ 924-5246 🚇 Houston St
🚌 M20 🕐 brunch Sat 11am-3pm, Sun 10:30am-3:30pm; lunch Mon-Fri noon-3pm; dinner Sun-Mon 6-10:30pm, Tues-Thurs 6-11:30pm, Fri 5:30pm-midnight, Sat 5:45pm-midnight ♿ [V]

La Petite Abeille (3, E3) $$

Belgian
It's Meatpacking District outside (cobblestone street and Meat Supermarket), but homey Belgian café inside, with checked tablecloths (blue and white) and floor (black and white), Tin Tin on the walls, a wine list on the chalkboard and a menu that features croque monsieur, salads, mussels, roast chicken and beef stew.
✉ 400 W 14th St at Hudson St ☎ 727-1505
🚇 14th St-8th Ave
🚌 M14 🕐 7am-4pm & 5-11pm ♿

Muffins, mochas, magazines: the laid-back café life

Angus Oborn

Magnolia Bakery
(3, F3) $
Bakery
The only thing that prevents these cupcakes from going straight from oven to tummy is the need to slather them with half an inch of icing on the way. Join the melee and line up for your own fluffy, heavenly bite.
✉ 401 Bleecker St at W 11th St ☎ 462-2572 🚇 14th St-8th Ave 🚌 M14, M20 ⏰ 10am-11:30pm (Fri-Sat to 12:30am) ♿ Ⅴ

Menu (3, E3) $$$
Modern French
Chef Julian Clauss-Ehlers doles out foodie prix fixe menus like On the Edge (with roast squab pigeon on a puree of sun chokes and quince sauce) and Comfort (smooth corn soup and breaded chicken).
✉ 46 Gansevoort St at Greenwich St ☎ 675-5224 🚇 14th St-8th Ave 🚌 M14 ⏰ noon-3pm & 5:30-11:30pm (Fri-Sun to midnight) Ⅴ

Restaurant Reading
The most comprehensive restaurant guide is the *Zagat Survey*, available at bookstores all over the city, though its critical assessments about the city's more famous restaurants tend to be overly enthusiastic. Restaurant reviews also appear weekly in the *New York Press*, *Time Out New York* and the Friday *New York Times*.

Moustache (3, G4) $
Middle Eastern
Create your own 'pitza' or pick and mix a selection of salads. Everything is fresh and herby.
✉ 90 Bedford St btw Grove & Barrow Sts (also at 265 E 10th St) ☎ 229-2220 🚇 Christopher St, Houston St ⏰ noon-midnight ♿ Ⅴ

Risotteria (3, G4) $
Italian
Obsessive perfectionism is nice when someone else is making the risotto. At this stylish but quite cheap shop-front spot, step up to the counter and pick from

three types of rice and myriad flavorful additions.
✉ 270 Bleecker St at Morton St ☎ 924-6664 🚇 W 4th St, Christopher St-Sheridan Sq ⏰ noon-11pm (Thurs-Sat to midnight) ♿ Ⅴ

Trattoria (3, G4) $$
Italian
An amiable bistro with pressed-tin ceilings, a wood floor and plenty of panache, Trattoria serves honest pasta and a litany of fish staples and specials reeled off rapid-fire by your waiter.
✉ 262 Bleecker St at Morton St ☎ 645-2993 🚇 W 4th St ⏰ noon-midnight ♿ Ⅴ

HARLEM

Sisters (1, C6) $
Caribbean
At this unprepossessing eatery, you sit down to eat in the glow of the TV and family photos. The rotis and curries are delicious (and huge), the side dishes (collard greens and plantain) are yummy, and the breakfasts (sautéed codfish, eggs 'n' grits) are as downhome as you get.
✉ 47 E 124th St at Madison Ave ☎ 410-3000 🚇 125th St (4, 5, 6) 🚌 M35, M101, M103 ⏰ 9am-8pm (Thurs-Sat to 9pm) ♿ Ⅴ

Spoonbread (2, A3) $$
Southern
Stop here if you've got an appetite for big plates of fried chicken, ribs and catfish with sides like cornbread, black-eyed peas and collard greens. Spoonbread, by the way, is a kind of cornbread soufflé, so moist it has to be ladled from the dish.
✉ 366 W 110th St btw Amsterdam & West End Aves (also Spoonbread Too, 547 Lenox Ave) ☎ 865-6744 🚇 Cathedral Pkwy ⏰ 10am-10pm ♿

Sylvia's (1, C5) $$
Southern
Sylvia Woods has run this restaurant for 40 years, and she's still packing them in. Local and tourists come in hungry for fried chicken, smothered pork chops, macaroni and cheese and other comfort food faves. Some of the sides (pinto beans, collard greens) are even available in cans to take home.
✉ 328 Lenox Ave btw 126th & 127th Sts ☎ 996-0660 🚇 125th St (2, 3) ⏰ Mon-Sat 8am-10:30pm, Sun 11am-8pm ♿

LITTLE ITALY/NOLITA

Cafe Gitane (3, H6) $
French

This smart retro café attracts the French, who bestow kisses left, right and center, and beautiful Australians, who go lighter on the smooching. With food that's elegant and delicious rather than hearty, Gitane makes a fabulous place for breakfast, salads, coffee and snacking on eye candy.

✉ 242 Mott St at Prince St ☎ 334-9552
⊜ Broadway-Lafayette St, Prince St, Spring St (6) ◷ 9am-midnight
♿ V

Cafe Habana (3, H6) $
Cuban

This cheap, hip Cuban diner offers filling food like tostadas, 'hamburgesas' and 'Tlacoyo tres Marias' (cornmeal cake stuffed with goat cheese and sun-dried tomatoes with chipotle salsa). Cold beer augments the buzz.

✉ 17 Prince St at Elizabeth St ☎ 625-2002 ⊜ Broadway-Lafayette St, Prince St, Spring St (6) ◷ noon-10pm ♿ V

Caffe Roma (3, J6) $
Café

This longstanding Little Italy hangout features atmosphere aplenty and an unhurried vibe – it's a good place to watch passersby from an outdoor table or to huddle indoors with granita, coffee or cannoli. Sit at a bench-style table and chat with a fellow cake eater.

✉ 385 Broome St at Mulberry St ☎ 226-8413 ⊜ Spring St (6), Bowery ◷ 8am-11:45pm ♿

Eight Mile Creek (3, H6) $$$
Australian

Kangaroo and emu are only the beginning of Australian food done Nolita style. Go for the hot and sour soup with cilantro dumplings and yabbie (Australian shellfish), the warm oyster pie or crispy squid.

✉ 240 Mulberry St btw Prince & Spring Sts ☎ 431-4635 ⊜ Broadway-Lafayette St, Prince St, Spring St (6) ◷ Tues-Sun 5:30-11pm (downstairs bar from noon Sat-Sun) V

Ghenet (3, H6) $$
Ethiopian

This classy restaurant (white tablecloths, recommended wines with each dish) raises the bar for Ethiopian cuisine. Along with injera (flat bread), foul (beans) and azifa (lentil salad), the menu includes American inflections like collard greens with marinated lamb.

✉ 284 Mulberry St btw Houston & Prince Sts ☎ 343-1888 ⊜ Broadway-Lafayette St, Prince St, Spring St (6) 🚌 M21 ◷ Mon 5-10:30pm, Tues-Sun noon-10:30pm V

Nyonya (3, J6) $
Malaysian

At this festive place, try sautéed frog and stingray, or opt for an array of less adventurous choices. The seafood dishes are mainly excellent – the specialty is jumbo prawns – and the noodle soups will fill you up till tomorrow.

✉ 194 Grand St btw Mott & Mulberry Sts ☎ 334-3669 ⊜ Grand St ◷ 11am-11:30pm ♿ V

Whichever Way You Slice It...

Ask a bunch of New Yorkers where to get the best pizza and you won't get a word in for a couple hours. The following parlors keep getting shout-outs from those who are particular about New York's classic thin-crust pies:

Grimaldi's (19 Old Fulton St, Brooklyn Heights; 3, M9; ☎ 718-858-4300; $) – coal-oven pizzas

John's Pizzeria (278 Bleecker St btw 6th & 7th Aves; 3, G4; ☎ 243-1680; $) – whole pies only

Lombardi's (32 Spring St at Mott St; 3, H6; ☎ 941-7994; $) – oldest parlor in town (1905)

Two Boots (42 Ave A at 3rd St; 3, G8; ☎ 254-1919; $) – classics, retreads, po' boys and calzones

LOWER EAST SIDE

Barrio (3, H8) $
Organic
Healthy without being too sprouty, the chemical-free food available here includes excellent omelets and hot sandwiches, served by cheery staff in an easy-going, faux-rustic setting. The under-stairs toilet is worth a visit.
✉ **99 Stanton St btw Orchard & Ludlow Sts** ☎ **533-9212** 🚇 **2nd Ave** 🚌 **M15** 🕐 **9am-2am** ⚭ **V**

Congee Village (3, J7) $
Chinese
Try terrific congee (soupy rice porridge), plain or with chicken, fish, abalone and even frog meat. Chinese people often start the day with a steaming bowl, but you can also have it later in the day. There's a wide selection of more recognizable Cantonese dishes, too.
✉ **100 Allen St at Delancey St** ☎ **941-1818** 🚇 **Delancey-Essex Sts** 🕐 **10:30am-midnight** ⚭

Grilled Cheese (3, H8) $
American
This tiny café applies the 'if you're going to do something, do it well' principle to toasted sandwiches. You build your own (starting at $3.50) or go for a pre-selected toastie. The 'Garden' ($6) crams sprouts, tomato and hummus into the goo. Wash it all down with a fruit smoothie.
✉ **168 Ludlow St at Stanton St** ☎ **982-6600** 🚇 **Delancey-Essex Sts** 🕐 **11am-11pm** ⚭ **V**

Lansky Lounge & Grill (3, H8) $$$
Modern American
Look for the 'L' to find the hidden entrance to this big spot, which contains a bar/lounge plus a restaurant that pushes 10oz cocktails, steaks, seafood and the obligatory raw bar offerings. Around 11pm, the tables are cleared away and a little booty gets shaken.
✉ **104 Norfolk St btw Rivington & Delancey Sts** ☎ **677-9489** 🚇 **Delancey-Essex Sts** 🕐 **6-11pm (Fri-Sat to midnight)**

Start the day right.

Angus Oborn

71 Clinton Fresh Food (3, H8) $$$
Modern American
Chef Wylie Dufresne brightens this starlet with dishes like scallops on olive-risotto cake or beer-braised ribs with garlic-mustard spaetzle. The no-cell-phone policy shouldn't trouble diners – everyone you'd want to talk to is already here.
✉ **71 Clinton St at Rivington St** ☎ **614-6960** 🚇 **2nd Ave, Delancey-Essex Sts** 🕐 **6-10pm (Fri-Sat to 11:30pm)**

Time Cafe (3, G6) $$
International
Though it looks like it might couple pretentious decor with mediocre food, Time turns out to be a winner. The varied menu runs from tapas to steak and pizza to quesadilla – whatever you pick, chances are it'll be really good. Eat outside under umbrellas or join the indoor hubbub.
✉ **380 Lafayette St at Great Jones St** ☎ **533-7000** 🚇 **Bleecker St** 🕐 **Mon-Fri 8am-midnight (Fri to 1am), Sat 10:30am-1am, Sun 10:30am-midnight**

Butts Out
Regulations forbid smoking in restaurants unless the management can satisfactorily separate smoke from nonsmokers – this means that smoking is banned in most restaurants. In warmer months, smokers can take advantage of New York's love affair with outdoor eating; in winter, ask if it's okay to smoke at the bar.

Perversely, while smoking has been shunned, cigar bars have become more popular. The **Fifty Seven Fifty Seven Bar** at the Four Seasons hotel (p. 104) offers cigars fresh from the humidor, as well as magic martinis.

LOWER MANHATTAN

Bridge Cafe
(3, M7) $$$
Modern American
Duck under the Brooklyn
Bridge into this exceedingly
congenial dining room in a
red-slatted homey haven
that's good for both a long
business lunch and a
romantic dinner. An excel-
lent wine list accompanies
the fine pasta, steak and
seafood fare. Reservations
recommended.
⊠ **279 Water St at
Dover St** ☎ **227-3344**
🚇 **City Hall** ⏲ **Sun-
Mon noon-10pm, Tues-
Thurs noon-11pm, Fri
noon-midnight, Sat
5pm-midnight** ♿

Mangia
(3, N6) $
Deli
Possibly the classiest lunch-
eonette in the city, Mangia
features salads with star
appeal, great soups (ask
for a sample) and tasty
sandwiches. Take it all back
to the trading floor or snag
a seat in a comfortable
banquette. Despite the Wall
St location, it's not outra-
geously expensive to grab
your lunch here.
⊠ **40 Wall St btw
William & Nassau Sts**
**(also at 50 W 57th St,
16 E 48th St)** ☎ **425-
4040** 🚇 **Wall St, Rector
St** ⏲ **Mon-Fri 7am-6pm**
♿ **V**

Paris Cafe
(3, M7) $$
Pub
Since 1873, this handsome
bar has hosted seamen,
fisherfolk and the famous
and notorious, including
Annie Oakley, Butch
Cassidy and the Sundance
Kid, Teddy Roosevelt and
members of the Murder Inc
crime gang of the 1930s.
Today, the crowd is more
low-key at this untouristy
spot that offers decent
food, heated foot rails and
plenty of atmosphere.
⊠ **119 South St at
Peck Slip** ☎ **240-9797**
🚇 **Fulton St** ⏲ **11am-
4am (kitchen closes
2am)**

Taking Care of Business
If you want to fête your clients with your lavish expense
account, try **La Côte Basque** (p. 79) or the **Four
Seasons** (below). For something less formal, consider
seafood tavern **City Crab** (235 Park Ave at E 19th St;
3, D6; ☎ 529-3800; $$$) or the **Wall St Kitchen &
Bar** (70 Broad St at Beaver St; 3, N6; ☎ 797-7070; $$)
for finger food, pasta and 50 wines by the glass. Go
to **Delmonico's** (56 Beaver St at William St; 3, N6;
☎ 509-1144; $$$) to seal the deal.

Jennifer Steffey

MIDTOWN

Four Seasons
(2, M7) $$$$
Modern French
The eclectic Continental
cuisine and the gold-
colored dining rooms
designed by Philip Johnson
and Mies van der Rohe
make you feel like you're
either Sean Connery or a
Bond girl, classy as can be.
The menu and mood
change with the season;
the art by Picasso, Miró
and Larry Rivers stays up all

year. Reservations essential.
Jacket and tie required.
⊠ **99 E 52nd St at Park
Ave** ☎ **754-9494**
🚇 **59th St (4, 5, 6),
Lexington Ave (N, R)**
⏲ **Mon-Fri noon-2pm &
5-9:30pm, Sat 5-11pm**

Fred's
(2, K6) $$
Modern American
The snooty basement
bar/restaurant at Barney's
department store (p. 54)
complements the fashion

upstairs. Fortify yourself for
another assault on the racks
with pasta, salads, melts or
dainty pizzas. Or, if you've
already shopped and are
about to drop, Fred's is the
perfect spot to contemplate
your Barney's purchases.
⊠ **10 E 61st St at
Madison Ave** ☎ **833-
2200** 🚇 **59th St (4, 5,
6), Lexington Ave (N, R)**
⏲ **Mon-Sat 11:30am-
8:30pm, Sun 11am-
6pm V**

Kangsuh Korean Restaurant (2, P5) $$

Korean

This hospitable two-story Korean stop fries up a mean kimchi, does lots of sushi and combines the two in a great dish called 'Hwe Dup Bob,' a salad of raw fish marinated in sesame oil and vegetables over rice.
✉ 1250 Broadway at W 32nd St ☎ 564-6845 Ⓢ Herald Sq ⏲ 24hrs ♿

La Côte Basque (2, L6) $$$$

French

Opened in 1957, this remains one of the city's finest dining experiences. Enjoy exquisite food in a luxurious setting with amiable hosts. The prix fixe menu sticks to the French classics but is no less delightful for that. Reservations essential. Jacket required.
✉ 60 W 55th St btw 5th & 6th Aves ☎ 688-6525 Ⓢ 5th Ave (E, F), 51st St ⏲ Mon-Sat noon-2:30pm & 5:30-10:30pm (Fri-Sat to 11:30pm), Sun 5:30-9:30pm (closed Sun in summer)

Reuben's (2, O6) $

American

Winning orange vinyl benches distinguish this old-style diner. The menu offers a fine choice of roasts, cold cuts and sandwiches, including the famous Reuben sandwich (invented here): corned beef, sauerkraut and Swiss cheese on rye. Or chow down on one of the top-notch, triple-decker celebrity sandwiches.
✉ 244 Madison Ave at E 38th St ☎ 867-7800 Ⓢ Grand Central-42nd St ⏲ Mon-Fri 6am-9:30pm, Sat 7am-4pm ♿

Waterside dining at Rockefeller Center

Esbin-Anderson Photography

Russian Tea Room (2, L5) $$$

Russian

At this revamped classic, the modernist Russian kitsch includes ice sculptures and an aquarium in the shape of a bear. Turn it all into a blur with house-infused vodkas (try the 'four alarm/five pepper'). Celebrities come to gorge on borscht and blinis.
✉ 150 W 57th St btw 6th & 7th Aves ☎ 974-2111 Ⓢ 57th St (N, R) ⏲ noon-3pm (Sat-Sun from 11am) & 5-10pm (Sat-Sun to 11pm) ♿

Soup Kitchen International (2, L4) $

Soup

The proprietor was made famous as the 'Soup Nazi' on *Seinfeld*, and that show was telling it like it is: you'd better know what you want – and have your money ready – by the time you reach the head of the line. The tasty soups are worth the rigor.
✉ 259a W 55th St at 8th Ave ☎ 757-7730 Ⓢ 7th Ave (B, D, E) ⏲ Mon-Fri noon-5:30pm (closed in summer) ♿ Ⓥ

Dinner before Drama

W 46th St between 8th and 9th Aves is known as Restaurant Row (2, N4), a strip that specializes in pre-theater dining. A lot of places rely on a rushed, captive audience, but there are a few standouts. **Pomaire** (371 W 46th St; ☎ 956-3056; $$) serves tasty Chilean food and does a prix fixe dinner that includes the namesake pomaire (clay-pot) stews. **Orso** (322 W 46th St; ☎ 489-7212; $$$) offers classy pizzas and Tuscan entrees but no prix fixe menu. **Joe Allen** (326 W 46th St; ☎ 581-6464; $$) is a little cheaper and more casual – it's always packed pre-show. **Barbetta** (321 W 46th St; ☎ 246-9171; $$$) is a charming, older-style Italian restaurant.

SOHO & NOHO

Cafe Borgia II (3, H5) $
Café
In this dim heart-of-Soho café, you can canoodle over strudel, some good coffee and decent toasted sandwiches, quiches and omelets. Sit at the sidewalk tables if you want to breathe fresh air and see a parade of gallery trawlers.
✉ **161 Prince St btw W Broadway & Thompson Sts** ☎ **677-1850** ⊕ **Prince St (N, R), Broadway-Lafayette St** ⏱ **10am-midnight (Fri-Sat to 2am)** ♿ V

Classy Soho café

Cafe Noir (3, J5) $$
Moroccan
Loud in summer, denlike in winter, Noir features a Moroccanish menu with huge couscous platters (consider sharing), wraps, salad, lots of seafood and paella. There are tapas, too, if you're in the mood for nibbling rather than noshing.
✉ **32 Grand St at Thompson St** ☎ **431-7910** ⊕ **Canal St (A, C, E)** ⏱ **noon-4am** V

Cub Room (3, E5) $$
Modern American
A large restaurant, bar and lounge can accommodate it all: slow brunches, light lunches, big dinners or lively nightcaps. It's zoned, so you can hang with chic barflies, families or art-buying bankers. Everything is organic, from the cheeseburger on the kids' menu to the obligatory crusted salmon on the grown-ups' rap sheet.
✉ **183 Prince St at Sullivan St** ☎ **777-0030** ⊕ **Prince St (N, R), Broadway-Lafayette St** ⏱ **noon-10:30pm (Fri-Sat to 12:30am)** ♿ V

Hampton Chutney Co (3, H6) $
New Indian
Get your dose of Hampton Chutney's dosas – modern reworkings of south India's thin pancakes folded over hot fillings. The classic spiced potato is available, but most offerings fall along more American lines, with jack cheese, arugula, grilled chicken and turkey.
✉ **68 Prince St btw Lafayette & Crosby Sts** ☎ **226-9996** ⊕ **Prince St (N, R), Broadway-Lafayette St** ⏱ **Mon-Sat 11am-8pm, Sun 11am-6pm** V

Other Foods (3, F6) $$
International
This classy café features white tablecloths, French doors and modern organic food, mostly locally grown or raised. The largely vegetarian menu makes an exception for white meats. The sandwiches (11am-5pm) explode with fresh ingredients. Later, there's always a fish, pasta, pizza and soup of the day.
✉ **47 E 12th St btw Broadway & University Pl** ☎ **358-0103** ⊕ **Union Sq** ⏱ **Mon-Sat 11am-10:30pm, Sun 11am-10pm** V

Palachinka (3, J5) $
Café
At this Soho fringe café, you can linger over a crêpe, ciabatta, salad or drink (great coffee!) at a chrome table or in the comfy anti-sidewalk-watching window bench. It's classy down to the details – even the toilet paper is groovy – but you get the feeling that aesthetic delight motivated the designers, rather than purposeful trendiness.
✉ **28 Grand St btw 6th Ave & Thompson St** ☎ **625-0362** ⊕ **Canal St (A, C, E)** ⏱ **10:30am-11pm (Thurs-Sat to 11:30pm)** ♿ V

Spring Street Natural (3, H6) $$
Vegetarian
Unprocessed, mostly organic ingredients turn into excitingly – but not preachingly – healthy cuisine. The mostly vegetarian menu ventures into chicken and fish, and – horrors! – there's a decent wine list. The large space can get loud, but the attentive waiters will always find you in the hubbub and serve you up food that's decidedly above par.
✉ **62 Spring St at Lafayette St** ☎ **966-0290** ⊕ **Spring St (6)** ⏱ **11:30am-11:30pm (Fri-Sat to 1am)** ♿ V

TRIBECA

Bubby's (3, K5)   **$$**
American
This big, breezy eatery has become an alarmingly popular spot for weekend brunches. It's also a good bet for salads, sandwiches, pastas and New York's best burger (or so they say – watch the 'wup-ass' sauce). Kids get crayons and balloons; those under age eight eat free on weekends 6-10pm.
✉ 120 Hudson St at N Moore St ☎ 219-0666 🄶 Franklin St ⏰ Mon-Thurs 8am-11pm, Fri 8am-midnight, Sat 9am-midnight, Sun 9am-10pm ♿ V

Chanterelle
(3, K5) $$$$
French
Extravagant prix fixe meals take care of your eating choices so you can concentrate on wooing your dinner partner at this romantic French restaurant with a downtown edge and seriously good food. The seafood sausage is a perennial favorite, and the cheese platters are sublime. Reservations essential.
✉ 2 Harrison St at Hudson St ☎ 966-6960

🄶 Franklin St
⏰ lunch Tues-Sat noon-2:30pm, dinner Mon-Sat 5:30-11pm

Le Zinc (3, L5)   **$$**
French
This hip newcomer is the budget brother of super-swank Chanterelle. Dine on flawless French fare sans guilt – it's a faux pas to skip the delectable corn-cakes – or just park at the bar and drink in the artsy gallery posters on the walls.
✉ 139 Duane St btw Church & W Broadway ☎ 513-0001 🄶 Chambers St ⏰ noon-4am

Nobu (3, K5)   **$$$**
Japanese
Bafflingly good food, a spectacular setting and celebrity cachet (Robert de Niro is part owner) ensure that Nobu is booked up a month in advance for dinner. (The adjoining Next Door Nobu doesn't take reservations.) Planning ahead or waiting in line is worth the effort: we had the meal of our lives here.
✉ 105 Hudson St at Franklin St ☎ 219-0500 🄶 Franklin St

⏰ lunch Mon-Fri 11:45am-2:15pm, dinner nightly 5:45-10:15pm; Next Door Nobu: Mon-Sat 5:45pm-midnight (Fri-Sat to 1am), Sun 5:45-11pm

Designer diner

Odeon (3, L5)   **$$**
Modern American
This fab, fancy diner buzzes with a smart crowd eating American meals with designer dabs (truffle oil, wild mushrooms and dehydrated tomatoes). Check out the art deco details. There's a special kids menu.
✉ 145 W Broadway at Thomas St ☎ 233-0507 🄶 Chambers St (1, 2, 3, 9, C) ⏰ 11:30am-2am ♿ V

Angus Oborn

Eating with Kids

Though New York restaurateurs rarely forbid children accompanied by their parents, most don't bend over backwards to accommodate the young and hungry. High chairs, booster seats and kids' menus are the exception rather than the rule in restaurants, though diners are usually welcoming, casual dining places. For family eating, it's best to book fine dining establishments ahead. These places welcome families: **EJ's Luncheonette** (p. 83), **Bubby's** (p. 81), **Cub Room** (p. 80), **Odeon** (p. 81) and **Brother Jimmy's** (p. 82).

Kim Grant

UPPER EAST SIDE

Brother Jimmy's (2, E7) $$
Southern
BBQ ribs and wings, prawns by the bucket and lashings of beer – it ain't classy but it's easygoing at this sports bar that welcomes kids (they eat free). Lots of specials include all-you-can-eat-and-drink evenings.
✉ 1644 3rd Ave at 92nd St ☎ 426-2020 🚇 96th St (4, 5, 6) 🚌 M101-103 ⏰ Mon-Fri 5pm-4am, Sat-Sun noon-4am (kitchen closes Mon-Thurs midnight, Fri-Sat 1am, Sun 11pm) ♿

Daniel (2, K7) $$$$
French
Old world la-di-da gets a little flirty at Daniel Boulud's lavish restaurant. Ancient mosaics and frescoes always make food taste better, don't you find? If you stretch belly and budget to the tasting menus, you'll get a feel for the all-around culinary genius of the man. Reservations recommended. Jacket required.
✉ Mayfair Hotel, 60 E 65th St at Park Ave ☎ 288-0033 🚇 68th

St ⏰ lunch Tues-Sat noon-2pm (no Sat lunch Jul-Aug), dinner Mon-Sat 5:45-11pm (Fri-Sat from 5:30pm) Ⓥ

Lexington Candy Shop (2, F7) $
American
Don't pass this classic diner by. School kids slurp up malteds and gossip, neighborhood folk nurse a coffee or a famed fresh lemonade, wannabes soak up the Robert Redford vibe (*Three Days of the Condor* was filmed here) and visitors try to look local by talking baseball over their burgers.
✉ 1226 Lexington Ave at 83rd St ☎ 288-0057 🚇 86th St (4, 5, 6) 🚌 M101-103 ⏰ Mon-Sat 7am-7pm, Sun 9am-6pm ♿ Ⓥ

Park View at the Boathouse (2, H5) $$$
Modern American
Most alluring in the sunny months, when you can nibble outdoors with half an eye on the boaters, this spot also makes a good stop in winter, when the dining room crackles with a wood fire. The food is

interesting and varied but doesn't always live up to the setting. Reservations recommended.
✉ The Boathouse in Central Park, 72nd St at East Dr ☎ 517-2233 🚇 77th St ⏰ lunch Mon-Fri 11:30am-3:30pm, Sat-Sun 11am-4pm; dinner 5:30-10pm (Fri-Sat to 11pm) ♿

Sarabeth's (2, E6) $$
American
Famous for brunch (go for 'Goldie Lox,' scrambled eggs with salmon and cream cheese), Sarabeth's is just as lovely for lunch, afternoon tea or dinner. High tea (served weekdays 3:30-5:30pm) is all elegant chitchat until you start chugging back the cakes. Reservations recommended for dinner.
✉ 1295 Madison Ave at 92nd St (also at the Whitney Museum) ☎ 410-7335 🚇 96th St (6) 🚌 M1-4 ⏰ Mon-Sat 8am-10:30pm, Sun 8am-9:30pm

Wu Liang Ye (2, F7) $$
Chinese
This uptown gem rescues New York's Sichuan cuisine from home delivery hell. Start with cold noodles or dumplings, then move onto seafood (conch and prawn dishes are good) or the tea-smoked duck. If you're looking for something lean, try the lunch specials and low-fat steamed dishes.
✉ 215 E 86th St at 3rd Ave ☎ 534-8899 🚇 86th St (4, 5, 6) 🚌 M86 ⏰ Mon-Fri 11:30am-10:30pm, Sat-Sun noon-10:30pm ♿ Ⓥ

The fish can practically jump out of the water onto plates at Central Park.

Eshin-Anderson Photography

UPPER WEST SIDE

Cafe con Leche
(2, G3) **$$**
Creole
Spicy dishes come your way fast at this easygoing neighborhood place that specializes in eggy breakfasts, chicken and seafood, plus a good variety of vegetarian dishes. The feisty paella feeds one or two. This is a comfortable spot to eat solo and a convivial place to eat with a group.
✉ **424 Amsterdam Ave btw 80th & 81st Sts** ☎ **595-7000** Ⓜ **79th St, 81st St** 🚌 **M79** ⏱ **8:30am-11pm (Thurs-Sat to midnight)** ♿ Ⓥ

EJ's Luncheonette
(2, G3) **$$**
American
This contrived 'classic' diner offers excellent food, dreamy shakes and friendly service. Lines stretch out the door for weekend brunches. Try 'Crunchy French Toast' (with almonds and Cornflakes), an odd-sounding winner. Blue Plate dinner specials are the way to go at the other end of the day. High chairs are available.
✉ **447 Amsterdam Ave at W 81st St (also at 1271 3rd Ave, 432 6th Ave)** ☎ **873-3444** Ⓜ **79th St, 81st St** 🚌 **M79** ⏱ **Sun-Thurs 8am-12:30am, Fri-Sat 8:30am-10:30pm** ♿ Ⓥ

Isabella's
(2, G4) **$$**
Modern American
This self-consciously classy restaurant does brunches, lunches, sunset snacks and dinners with the seafood, grills and salads that satisfy uptown's six-pack tummies.

Settle in the pleasant, spacious indoor area or go for the shady sidewalk seating. Reservations recommended Friday to Sunday night. No brunch reservations taken.
✉ **359 Columbus Ave at W 77th St** ☎ **724-2100** Ⓜ **81st St** 🚌 **M7, M11, M79** ⏱ **Mon-Fri 11:30am-12:30am, Sat 11am-1am, Sun 10am-midnight**

La Caridad
(2, G3) **$**
Cuban-Chinese
This great cuisine mix means you get 'Chop Suey de Pollo' and 'Egg Foo Young de Jamon,' plus bean soup and sweet and sour plantains. Don't come for the atmosphere – it's a canteen setup with brutal lighting and overenthusiastic climate control. Do come for the food – it's simply good. You'll get enough to share.
✉ **2199 Broadway at W 78th St** ☎ **874-2780** Ⓜ **79th St** 🚌 **M79** ⏱ **Mon-Sat 11:30am-midnight, Sun 11:30am-10:30pm** ♿ Ⓥ

Ollie's
(2, F3) **$**
Chinese
The idea is 'Mott St on Broadway,' which seems to mean diner-style Chinese modified for the western (as in, Upper West Side) palate. Highlights of the huge menu are the all-day dim sum and meal-size soups. This makes a fine stop for the kids.
✉ **2315 Broadway at W 84th St** ☎ **362-3111** Ⓜ **86th St (1, 9)** ⏱ **11:30am-midnight (Fri-Sat to 1am)** ♿ Ⓥ

Saigon Grill
(2, F3) **$$**
Vietnamese
This tasty and popular neighborhood eatery has a large menu that starts at savory crystal dumplings and doesn't take a breath till 'Grandma's Sweet Rice Dumplings.' The standouts along the way are seafood bouillabaisse and curry okra. Reservations recommended.
✉ **2381 Broadway at W 87th St** ☎ **875-9072** Ⓜ **86th St (1, 9)** 🚌 **M86** ⏱ **11am-midnight** ♿ Ⓥ

It's Research!
Pretend you're writing a novel while you spy on the passing parade at these places. **Pick Me Up** (145 Ave A at E 9th St; 3, F8; ☎ 673-7231; $) is a lovely spot to linger and chew on a pen. With the help of strudel and cream, try your hand at penning a political saga at the **Hungarian Pastry Shop** (1030 Amsterdam Ave at W 111th St; 2, A3; ☎ 866-4230; $). Grapple with existential musings at **La Goulue** (746 Madison Ave at E 65th St; 2, K6; ☎ 988-8169; $$), where the meaning of life is revealed through fashion. Budding scriptwriters can workshop at the **Tribeca Grill** (375 Greenwich St at Franklin St; 3, K4; ☎ 941-3900; $$$), downstairs from Robert de Niro's office and prime star-spotting territory.

entertainment

New York's novella-length weekly entertainment listings tend to include a favorite performer you never dared dream you'd see live, half a dozen legendary ensembles, at least one musician you thought was dead, and hundreds of acts that you haven't heard of – in all, a tantalizing mixture, encompassing just about every form of performance imaginable. The city also contains thousands of venues, ranging from poky bars to pulsating nightclubs, where you can create your own party.

Information Lines

NYC On Stage ☎ 768-1818 – comprehensive theater, music and dance listings

Clubfone ☎ 777-2582 – selective club, live music, dance and cabaret information

Culture Finder e www.culturefinder .com – a good resource for all sorts of goings-on

The Broadway Line ☎ 302-4111, 888-276-2392 – theater information

Broadly speaking, **Soho** is the place to go for trendy lounges and bar/restaurants, while **Greenwich Village** boasts the best concentration of live music venues, student hangouts and gay bars. Hip bars and dance clubs have partly taken over the adjoining **Meatpacking District**. A volatile mix of mainstream and hardcore clubs and lounges, **Chelsea** draws mixed crowds. Above a residue of grungy bars, the **East Village** features a top layer of fashionable hideouts. You'll find an upscale after-work scene in **Midtown**, a sprinkling of student hangouts and ritzy lounges on the **Upper West Side** and a mix of dives and jazz and gospel venues in **Harlem**.

To find out about high culture happenings, see the Friday and Sunday *New York Times* and the weekly *New Yorker*. For clubs and live music listings, see the free weekly *Village Voice* and *New York Press*. The *Voice* and the weekly *Time Out New York* magazine both have extensive gay listings. The monthly magazines *Paper*, *411* and *Flyer* give the lowdown on clubs and parties. *Free Time* is an excellent monthly guide to free or cheap goings-on around town.

Get your tickets here: TKTS, Times Square

Kim Grant

SPECIAL EVENTS

January *Three Kings Parade* – Jan 5; kids' parade along 5th Ave to Spanish Harlem

Chinese New Year – fireworks and parades in and around Chinatown

Black History Month – African American history and culture events

March *St Patrick's Day Parade* – Mar 17; huge Irish march down 5th Ave

May *Long Island City Art Frenzy* – mid-month; arts festival in Queens

Fleet Week – late May; annual gathering of sailors, naval ships and air rescue teams

Carnaval – Memorial Day weekend; celebration of Hispanic culture

June *JVC Jazz Festival* – mid- to late June; concerts by top names in jazz at all concert halls in town

NY Shakespeare Festival – three months of free performances in Central Park

Lesbian & Gay Pride Week – late June; parade down 5th Ave and many other events in Greenwich Village

July *Independence Day* – Jul 4; celebrations throughout the city

Lincoln Center Festival – monthlong performances by international actors, singers and acrobats (includes free events)

Central Park Concerts – under-the-stars performances by the New York Philharmonic and the Metropolitan Opera

August *Harlem Week* – a 'week' that takes the whole month to celebrate Harlem's history and culture

Charlie Parker Jazz Festival – late Aug; outdoor shows in the East Village and Harlem

US Open Tennis Tournament – late Aug; premier tennis tournament at the National Tennis Center (p. 102) in Flushing Meadows, Queens

September *Downtown Arts Festival* – visual and performing arts events in Chelsea and Soho over three weeks

Caribbean Day – early Sept; huge Brooklyn Parade

San Gennaro – mid-Sept; Little Italy fiesta with a parade led by the effigy of San Gennaro, the patron saint of Naples

New York Film Festival – late Sept to mid-Oct; a major event at Lincoln Center

October *Halloween Parade* – Oct 31; wild and colorful march down 6th Ave in Greenwich Village

November *New York Marathon* – early Nov; road race through all five boroughs

Macy's Thanksgiving Day Parade – 4th Thurs; balloons and floats paraded down Broadway from W 72nd St to Herald Square

Rockefeller Center Christmas Tree Lighting – late Nov; start of the Christmas season, with celebrity performances and the Radio City Music Hall Rockettes

December *New Year's Eve* – Dec 31; Times Square festivities, 5-mile midnight run in Central Park, fireworks at South Street Seaport

Angus Oborn

THEATER

Circle in the Square Theatre (2, M5)
This off-Broadway non-profit theater staged groundbreaking productions, such as Eugene O'Neill's *The Iceman Cometh*, at its original 159 Bleecker St premises (which now hosts performances by New School students). The company is actively involved in New York's thespian scene, not least through its theater school.
✉ **1633 Broadway at 50th St** ☎ **307-2705, Telecharge 239-6200** |e| **www.circlesquare .org** Ⓣ **50th St (1, 9)**

Eugene O'Neill Theater (2, M4)
This pleasant 1100-seat theater has a fine history of top theatrical productions

like Neil Simon's *A Thousand Clowns* and *Prisoner of Second Avenue* and Arthur Miller's *All My Sons*. Recent shows include a genitalia-free *Full Monty*.
✉ **230 W 49th St btw Broadway & 8th Ave** ☎ **Telecharge 239-6200** Ⓣ **49th St, 50th St (1, 9)**

Flea Theater (3, K5)
This Tribeca theater tends to host unconventional drama and dance companies that can cope with the space: the smallish audience is on the same level as the performers and creative staging is a necessity.
✉ **41 White St btw Broadway & Church St** ☎ **226-2407** Ⓣ **Franklin St**

Joseph Papp Public Theater (3, G6)
Founded in 1954, this is one of the city's most important cultural centers. Meryl Streep, Robert de Niro and Kevin Kline have performed here. The theater hosts the free New York Shakespeare Festival at Central Park's Delacorte Theater. It also runs Joe's Pub, a plush cabaret hall next door.
✉ **425 Lafayette St at Astor Pl** ☎ **539-8500, Telecharge 239-6200** |e| **www.publictheater .org** Ⓣ **Astor Pl** ♿

The Kitchen (3, D2)
Over 30 years here, artists like Philip Glass, Laurie Anderson, David Byrne, Peter Greenaway, Brian Eno, Robert Mapplethorpe and Cindy Sherman have put on performances of the everything-but-the-sink variety. Expect to see anything from new-wave trapeze to video installations.
✉ **512 W 19th St btw 10th & 11th Aves** ☎ **255-5793** |e| **www .thekitchen.org** Ⓣ **14th St-8th Ave**

Majestic Theatre (2, N4)
Probably Broadway's best theater, the Majestic boasts a history of blockbuster musicals like *Carousel*, *South Pacific* and *Camelot*. It's now hosting *The Phantom of the Opera*, probably until the sky falls down. Most of its 1600 seats offer good views. Kids are welcome.
✉ **247 W 44th St at 8th Ave** ☎ **Telecharge 239-6200** Ⓣ **42nd St-Times Sq** Ⓢ **$35-85** ♿

Buying Tickets
Ticketmaster (☎ 307-4100; |e| www.ticketmaster .com) and **Telecharge** (☎ 239-6200; |e| www.tele charge.com) sell tickets to most major concerts and sporting events.

Ticket Central (416 W 42nd St btw 9th & 10th Aves; 2, L4; ☎ 279-4200) handles Broadway and off-Broadway theater tickets. For Broadway performances, visit the **Broadway Ticket Center** (Times Square Visitors' Center, 1560 Broadway btw 46th & 47th Sts; 2, N5; ◷ Mon-Sat 9am-7pm, Sun 10am-6pm).

The Times Square **TKTS** booth (Broadway at W 47th St; 2, N5; ☎ 768-1818) sells same-day tickets at up to 50% off (evening tickets: Mon-Sat 3-8pm, Sun 11am-8pm; matinee tickets: Wed & Sat 10am-2pm). Credit cards aren't accepted. At press time, the TKTS booth from the World Trade Center had relocated to Bowling Green Plaza (Whitehall St; 3, O5; ◷ Mon-Fri 11am-5:30pm, Sat 11am-3:30pm).

Visit box offices for rush and standing-room tickets, usually released on the day of performance only. At about 6pm, ask if there are any unclaimed VIP, press or cast tickets available.

New Victory Theatre
(2, O5) Home to high-energy family-friendly productions from around the world, this theater has hosted everything from Australia's Flying Fruit Fly Circus to The Netherlands' Runt, featuring 28 dog puppets. Families can also find plenty of entertainment at the Disney-owned New Amsterdam Theatre (214 W 42nd St), across the street.
✉ **209 W 42nd St & Broadway** ☎ **382-4000, Telecharge 239-6200**
e www.newvictory.org
Ⓜ 42nd St-Times Sq ♿

Performing Garage
(3, J5) An off-Broadway theater founded in 1967, this is still one of the most consistent of the avant-garde performance spaces. It's home to the Wooster Group, whose members have included such famous names as Willem Dafoe, Spalding Gray and Steve Buscemi.
✉ **33 Wooster St btw Broome & Grand Sts**
☎ **966-3651** Ⓜ **Canal St (A, C, E, 1, 9)**

PS122 (3, F7)
Since its inception in 1979, this off-off-Broadway dance and theater space has been committed to fostering new artists and their way-out ideas. Its two stages have hosted Eric Bogosian, Meredith Monk, Penny Arcade and a hip-hop theater festival.
✉ **150 1st Ave at E 9th St** ☎ **477-5829, box office 477-5288**
e www.ps122.org, tickets: www.ticketweb .com Ⓜ 1st Ave
🚌 **M15**

The new, family-friendly face of Times Square

COMEDY

Caroline's (2, M5)
This cellar room seats 350 for stylish supper-club eats and giggles. It's a slick, rather than intimate, place, but you can rely on pretty good, mostly mainstream laughs. There's a bar to escape to if your funny bone isn't being tickled.
✉ **1626 Broadway at 49th St** ☎ **757-4100**
e www.carolines.com
Ⓜ 50th St (1, 9)
🕐 shows nightly from 7:30pm, Sat-Sun 2pm
$ **$15-35 & 2-drink minimum**

Comedy Cellar (3, G5)
This long-running comedy club showcases high-profile comics well known from TV chat shows, sitcoms and cable comedy specials. The Cellar has a history of surprise guests like Robin Williams, Steven Wright and Jerry Seinfeld.
✉ **117 MacDougal St btw W 3rd & Bleecker Sts** ☎ **254-3480**
e www.comedycellar .com Ⓜ W 4th St
🕐 9pm-2:30am
$ **$10-12 & 2-drink minimum (free tickets available on website)**

Gotham Comedy Club (3, D5)
This medium-size stand-up club doesn't have the star power of some of the more established venues, but if you come here, you can say, 'I saw him when he was Joe Nobody in New York City' in a few years.
✉ **34 W 22nd St btw 5th & 6th Aves** ☎ **367-9000** **e** www.gotham comedy.citysearch.com
Ⓜ 5th Ave (N, R)
🕐 shows from 8:30pm
$ **$10-15 & 2-drink minimum**

Stand-Up New York
(2, G3) You need to reserve your spot at this popular uptown laugh-den. Theme nights like 'Funny Bitches' and 'Southern-Fried Humor' draw the crowds, as do the promise of surprise appearances from star comedians.
✉ **236 W 78th St at Broadway** ☎ **595-0850**
Ⓜ 79th St 🕐 shows 6 & 9pm (plus 8pm, 10pm & 12:15am Fri-Sat)
$ **$10 ($12 Fri-Sat) & 2-drink minimum**

CLASSICAL MUSIC, OPERA & DANCE

Amato Opera Theater (3, G6)

This small but tenacious company has been going for more than 50 years and remains just as ambitious as ever; it's a proving ground for the city's up-and-coming singers. The stage is tiny – 20ft (6m) wide – but 70 performers have been crammed onto it.
✉ **319 Bowery at 2nd St** ☎ 228-8200
e www.amato.org
🚇 2nd Ave

Brooklyn Academy of Music (6, F2)

This excellent complex, which includes an opera house, playhouse and cinemas, hosts popular artists and experimental performers who nudge the mainstream, like Philip Glass, Laurie Anderson and the Kronos Quartet. In summer, concerts take place in the BAM café.
✉ **30 Lafayette Ave (cnr Flatbush & Atlantic Aves), Brooklyn**
☎ 718-636-4100
e www.bam.org
🚇 Atlantic Ave, Pacific St, Fulton St 🚌 BAMbus from 120 Park Ave at 42nd St 1hr prior to most performances
💲 varies; $10 student/senior rush tickets 2hrs before shows (cash only)

Carnegie Hall (2, L5)

Since it opened in 1891, everyone's appeared here: Tchaikovsky conducted the opening festival; Mahler and Prokofiev performed their own works; Fats Waller, Woody Guthrie, Miles Davis, the Beatles and the Rolling Stones have all taken the stage in the main or recital halls.
✉ **154 W 57th St at 7th Ave** ☎ 247-7800
e www.carnegiehall .org 🚇 57th St (N, R), 7th Ave (B, D, E) 💲 as low as $12 for nonsubscription events; cheap student tickets from box office 2hrs before some concerts

Chamber Music Society of Lincoln Center (2, J3)

Directed by clarinetist David Shifrin, the Society is the foremost chamber music company in the US. The main concert series is in early autumn. Alice Tully Hall also hosts seasons of the New York Chamber Symphony.
✉ **Alice Tully Hall, W 65th St at Broadway, Lincoln Center** ☎ 875-5050, CenterCharge 721-6500 e www .chambermusicsociety .org 🚇 66th St-Lincoln Center

City Center of Music & Dance (2, L5)

This landmark theater hosts the Alvin Ailey American Dance Theatre every December, as well as engagements by the American Ballet Theatre and foreign companies. The Manhattan Theatre Club performs in smaller auditoriums onsite.
✉ **W 55th St btw 6th & 7th Aves** ☎ 247-0430, box office 581-1212 e www.city center.org 🚇 57th St (N, R), 7th Ave (B, D, E)

Dance Theatre of Harlem (north of 1, A3)

Founded in 1969, this neoclassical, mainly African American company is now recognized as one of the best in the world. The group's oft-reprised classics include *Firebird*, *South African Suite* and *The Prodigal Son*.
✉ **466 W 152nd St btw Amsterdam & St Nicholas Aves** ☎ 690-2800
e www.dancetheatre ofharlem.com 🚇 157th St 🚌 M3, M18, M100, M101

Joyce Theater (3, D3)

This offbeat dance venue seats 470 in a renovated cinema. The Erick Hawkins and Merce Cunningham dance companies are among those who have performed here. The foundation subsidizes most seasons at the theater, which enables noncommercial troupes to bring their work to an audience.
✉ **175 8th Ave at W 19th St** ☎ 242-0800
e www.joyce.org
🚇 18th St ♿

Juilliard School

One of America's foremost training academies for classical performance artists, the Juilliard School (W 66th St btw Amsterdam Ave & Broadway; 2, J3) was the only classical music college in the country when it was founded in 1905. Most of the 500 annual performances staged by students are free. Call ☎ 799-5000 to find out where and when.

Bargemusic

The intimate salon atmosphere, the romance of being on the river and the quality of the chamber music performances make Bargemusic a very special New York experience. It happens at the Fulton Ferry Landing, Brooklyn (3, M9). Call ☎ 718-624-4061 for a program and tickets.

Metropolitan Opera

(2, K3) A uniformly spectacular mixture of classics and premieres marks every season (September to April). It's nearly impossible to get into the first few performances of operas that feature big stars, but be patient: once the B team takes over, tickets become available.

✉ Amsterdam Ave btw W 62nd & 65th Sts, Lincoln Center ☎ 362-6000 |e| www.metopera.org 🅜 66th St-Lincoln Center

New York City Ballet

(2, K3) Established by Lincoln Kirstein and George Balanchine in 1948, the company performs a varied program of premieres and revivals; the yearly repertoire always includes *The Nutcracker* in the Christmas season.

✉ New York State Theater, W 62nd St at Columbus Ave, Lincoln Center ☎ 870-5570, CenterCharge 721-6500, student hotline 870-7766 |e| www.nycballet.com 🅜 66th St-Lincoln Center

New York City Opera

(2, K3) Emerging, enthusiastic singers (who just might be the Met stars of tomorrow) present daring and affordable performances of new works, neglected operas and revitalized standard repertory. The split season runs from September to November and from March to April.

✉ New York State Theater, W 62nd St at Columbus Ave, Lincoln Center ☎ 870-5630, box office 870-5570, Ticketmaster 307-4100 |e| www.nycopera.com 🅜 66th St-Lincoln Center

New York Philharmonic

(2, K3) One of the world's most distinguished orchestras, the Philharmonic has performed over 13,000 times since its founding in 1842. Maestro Lorin Maazel begins his tenure as music director in September 2002, taking over from the venerable Kurt Masur. Maazel first conducted the Philharmonic as a child prodigy in the 1940s.

✉ Avery Fisher Hall, W 65th St at Columbus Ave, Lincoln Center ☎ CenterCharge 721-6500, discount ticket information 875-5656 |e| www.newyorkphilharmonic.org 🅜 66th St-Lincoln Center

The dazzling Metropolitan Opera House at Lincoln Center

JAZZ & BLUES

Arthur's Tavern
(3, G4) A horn player may suddenly stand up beside you and blow your ear off at this tiny bar with a minuscule stage. There's jazz and blues every night and sing-along classics on the weekends.
✉ 57 Grove St at 7th Ave ☎ 675-6879
🚇 Christopher St
🕐 Sun-Mon 8pm-3am, Tues-Thurs 6:30pm-3am, Fri-Sat 6:30pm-3:30am ⑤ no cover; 1-drink minimum per set

BB King Blues Club & Grill (2, O4)
This flashy new 500-seater in the revitalized Times Square hosts the sublime (George Clinton, Etta James) and the ridiculous (Little River Band, Air Supply). There's food every night and a Sunday gospel brunch at 1pm.
✉ 237 W 42nd St btw 7th & 8th Aves
☎ information 997-4144, tickets 307-7171
🌐 www.bbkingblues.com 🚇 42nd St-Port Authority 🕐 shows usually at 8 & 10pm
⑤ $25-35

Blue Note (3, G4)
At New York's most famous (and expensive) jazz club, big stars do short sets. Some great music gets played here, which makes braving the thicket of tourists worth it. The onsite restaurant serves a lot of red meat and seafood. Blue Note members get special offers (join via the website).
✉ 131 W 3rd St at 6th Ave ☎ 475-8592
🌐 www.bluenote.net
🚇 W 4th St 🕐 6pm-1am (Fri-Sat to 2am); shows 9 & 11:30pm
⑤ usually $10-50; food $$$

Chicago Blues (3, E3)
Blues masters and up-and-coming baton carriers play seven nights a week in this none-too-flashy pub. If you've got a harmonica in your pocket, you can jump into the fray for Monday night's blues jam.
✉ 73 8th Ave at 14th St ☎ 924-9755
🌐 www.chicagoblues nyc.com 🚇 14th St-8th Ave 🕐 5pm-2am (Fri-Sat to 3am) ⑤ free-$20

Copeland's
(north of 1, A2) Feast on the soul food buffet every Sunday and enjoy a gospel choir at this touristy spot with decent performances. Tuesday to Sunday, come for dinner and a show, with a varied jazz program and a mostly Southern menu.
✉ 547 W 145th St btw Broadway & Amsterdam Ave ☎ 234-2356
🚇 145th St (1, 9)
🚌 M4, M5, M101, M102 🕐 Tues-Thurs 4:30-11pm, Fri-Sat 4:30pm-midnight, Sun noon-9pm ⑤ cover varies; food $$

Fez (3, G6)
This all-seats venue under the Time Cafe (p. 77) is a great place to see music. Fez hosts the wildly popular Mingus Big Band every Thursday. On other nights, you can catch cabaret, lounge music and rock.
✉ 380 Lafayette St at Great Jones St ☎ 533-2680, reservations 533-7000 🌐 www .feznyc.com 🚇 Bleecker St 🕐 6pm-2am (Fri-Sat to 4am)
⑤ $10-15 & 2-drink minimum; some student discounts

55 Bar (3, F4)
This authentic smoky jazz, blues and fusion joint features live music nightly from about 10pm. Expect sets by excellent resident artists, plus guest spots by the grand and unplanned.
✉ 55 Christopher St at 7th Ave ☎ 929-9883
🚇 Christopher St
🕐 8am-4am ⑤ cover $3-15

Got the blues? Head to Times Square.

Brad Jones and Dave Douglas jam at Iridium.

Iridium (2, M5)
This splashy club with way-out decor and good acoustics features quality trad jazz acts two sets a night during the week and a cooking three sets on weekends. A jazz brunch happens on Sunday, and the irrepressible Les Paul appears every Monday.
✉ **1650 Broadway at 51st St** ☎ **582-2121** **e** **www.iridiumjazz club.com** ⊕ **50th St (1, 9)** ⏲ **7pm-midnight (Fri-Sat to 2am); shows at 8:30pm & 10:30pm** ⑤ **$20-40**

Small's (3, F4)
This unique jazz cellar without a liquor license (free self-serve nonalcoholic drinks) hosts a 10hr jazz marathon every night from 10pm; it attracts top talent. After 4am, it's 'jam house' till dawn.
✉ **183 W 10th St at 7th Ave** ☎ **929-7565** **e** **www.smallsjazz .com** ⊕ **Christopher**

St-Sheridan Sq ⏲ **10pm-8am (Fri-Sun from 7:30pm)** ⑤ **jazz marathon $10**

St Nick's Pub
(north of 1, A4) Jazz jams on Monday and Wednesday nights draw a happy, mixed crowd to this Harlem hangout. Head to the garden out the back for 'tween-sets talk. Tuesday is comedy night.
✉ **773 St Nicholas Ave btw 148th & 149th Sts**

☎ **283-9728** ⊕ **145th St (A, B, C, D)** 🚌 **M3, M18** ⏲ **Sun-Fri noon-4am, Sat noon-3am** ⑤ **free-$3**

Village Vanguard
(3, F4) This basement-level venue may be the world's most prestigious jazz club; it's hosted literally every major star of the past 50 years. The cover charges aren't as hefty as those at the Blue Note.
✉ **178 7th Ave S at 11th St** ☎ **255-4037** **e** **www.village vanguard.net** ⊕ **Christopher St-Sheridan Sq** ⏲ **8:30pm-late** ⑤ **varies**

Wells Restaurant
(1, B5) Progressive jazz combos entertain on Friday, Saturday and Monday, and a relaxed jazz brunch draws music lovers on Sunday. Most folks take in dinner and a show, but you can just prop yourself at the bar and listen to the music.
✉ **2247 Powell Blvd at 133rd St** ☎ **234-0700** ⊕ **135th St (2, 3)** 🚌 **M2** ⏲ **11am-midnight (to 4am Fri-Sat)** ⑤ **varies**

The Big Apple

It was long thought that New York City was dubbed 'The Big Apple' by jazz musicians who regarded a gig in Harlem as a sure sign that they had made it to the top. But the term first appeared in the 1920s, when it was used by a journalist, John FitzGerald, who covered horse races for the *Morning Telegraph*. Apparently, stable hands at a New Orleans racetrack called a trip to a New York racetrack 'the Big Apple' – or greatest reward – for any talented thoroughbred. The slang stayed in popular usage long after the newspaper – and FitzGerald – disappeared.

ROCK, HIP-HOP, FOLK & WORLD MUSIC

Apollo Theater
(1, C4) Harlem's leading space for political rallies and concerts since 1914, the Apollo has hosted virtually every major black artist of note in the 1930s and '40s, including Duke Ellington, Bessie Smith, Billie Holiday and Charlie Parker. These days, most of the acts tend toward hip-hop and R&B. Wednesday's amateur night has launched Ella Fitzgerald, James Brown and, more recently, D'Angelo. It's fun for kids, too.
✉ 253 W 125th St at Frederick Douglass Blvd ☎ 749-5838, box office 531-5305 e www.its showtimeattheapollo .com ⊕ 125th St (A, B, C, D) 🚌 M2, M7, M10, M100, M102 ⑤ varies ♿

Arlene Grocery
(3, H8) Local music, student sagas and cheap beer heat things up every night and often make for some great entertainment. Look out for classic album nights (live renditions of records ranging from Rubber Soul to Weezer's Pinkerton), and don't miss the hilarious

The Apollo: Harlem's landmark club

punk-rock karaoke.
✉ 95 Stanton St at Orchard St ☎ 358-1633 e www.arlene grocery.com ⊕ 2nd Ave ⊙ 6pm-2am ⑤ free-$5

CBGB (OMFUG)
The prototypical punk club CBGB (315 Bowery at Bleecker St; 3, H6; ☎ 982-4052; e www.cbgb.com; ⊕ 2nd Ave), incubator of such famous acts as the Talking Heads and the Ramones, is still going strong after nearly three decades – it's one of the few places in New York that looks, feels and smells exactly like you imagined it would.

The elaborate name stands for Country, Bluegrass, Blues and Other Music for Uplifting Gourmandizers. The country only lasted for the first year – by 1974, the emphasis was rock. CBGB's 313 Gallery (☎ 677-0455), next door, presents acoustic music every night.

Bowery Ballroom
(3, J7) Popular touring acts like Smog, Dirty Three, Catpower and Stereo MCs have performed at this big atmospheric venue with a dungeonesque bar and a large gig hall that includes a balcony and make-out room.
✉ 6 Delancey St at Bowery ☎ 533-2111, tickets 269-4849 e www.bowery ballroom.com ⊕ Grand St, Bowery ⑤ $12-30

Brownies (3, F8)
This one-room indie haven suffers from a dodgy PA system and a grungy beer-soaked feel – which is all the better for the local and not-quite-famous touring bands that swing through. The Ben Folds Five, Elliot Smith and Jungle Brothers all played here before they hit it semi-big.
✉ 169 Ave A btw 10th & 11th Sts ☎ 420-8392 e www .browniesnyc.com ⊕ 1st Ave ⊙ 5pm-4am ⑤ around $10

Irving Plaza (3, E6)
Lots of fans don't mind standing up to hear well-known acts like Luscious Jackson, Femi Kuti, Calexico and Luka Bloom. Irving Plaza's presence has woken up a formerly sleepy neighborhood; the many bars that have popped up on 15th St attract an NYU college crowd.
✉ 17 Irving Pl at 15th St ☎ 777-6817, concert hotline 777-1224, Ticketmaster 307-4100 e www.irvingplaza .com ⊕ Union Sq ⑤ $15-30

Knitting Factory

(3, K5) This noise art space features alt-jazz, rock, hip-hop, Hasidic new wave, cosmic space jazz and whatever else is out there on the fringe, plus something traditional every now and then. Choose among four performance spaces: Alterknit, Old Office Lounge, the main space and a tap bar with free music nightly from 11pm.
✉ **74 Leonard St at Church St** ☎ **219-3006** e **www.knitting factory.com** 🚇 **Franklin St** 🕐 **4:30pm-late** 💲 **usually $8-15**

Luna Lounge (3, H8)

It's almost always free so it never hurts to poke your head in and see what's cooking at this hangout bar with a small room in the back for garage bands, local musicians and up-and-coming indie darlings. Monday night is comedy night, often featuring big-gish names testing out their new material.
✉ **171 Ludlow St btw Stanton & Houston Sts** ☎ **260-2323** 🚇 **2nd Ave** 🕐 **7:30pm-4am** 💲 **free; comedy $7**

World Music Institute

This organization (☎ 545-7536; e www.hearthe world.org) presents music from Afghanistan to Zimbabwe at various venues, including Washington Square Church (135 W 4th St; 3, G4; ☎ 777-2528) and Carnegie Hall (p. 88). There are usually two shows each weekend ($10-25).

Mercury Lounge

(3, H7) Ween, Radiohead and Lou Reed have all played at this smallish but comfortable venue, which blasts local and touring indie and rock music through its quality sound system every night.
✉ **217 E Houston St at Ave A** ☎ **260-4700, tickets 269-4849** e **www.mercury loungenyc.com** 🚇 **2nd Ave** 🚌 **M15, M21** 🕐 **7pm-late** 💲 **$8-20**

Pete's Candy Store

(6, E2) This bar offers live sets in its tiny band room out back and cocktails and grilled sandwiches up front. The free, eclectic music has included sets by Will Oldham, Nic Endo and Machine Translations. Tuesday is bingo night, and literary readings start at 7pm on Thursday.
✉ **709 Lorimer St, Williamsburg, Brooklyn** ☎ **718-302-3770** e **www.petescandy store.com** 🚇 **Lorimer St (L)** 🕐 **shows from 9pm** 💲 **free**

SOB's (3, H4)

Afro-Cuban sounds, hip-hop, salsa, reggae and even Indian bhangra, both live and on the turntable, make this place jump, especially in the wee hours (though there are also dinner shows nightly). Live acts (some Brazilian) take the stage till 2am, then give way to wild DJs and drummers. Saturday's late-night samba is a top party.
✉ **204 Varick St at W Houston St** ☎ **243-4940** e **www.sobs .com** 🚇 **Houston St** 🕐 **7pm-late** 💲 **$12-20**

Tonic (3, H8)

Minimalist John Zorn is a regular performer and curator at this interesting venue that showcases new music (jazz, electronic, underground, songwriter nights), plus films, offbeat theater and other eclectica.
✉ **107 Norfolk St btw Delancey & Rivington Sts** ☎ **358-7501** e **www.tonic107.com** 🚇 **Delancey-Essex Sts** 🕐 **noon-late** 💲 **usually around $10**

A moment of Motown in the Big Apple

CABARET

Cotton Club (1, B2)
One of old New York's veterans rides again as a touristy buffet-dinner-and-show venue. A changing program of swing, blues and jazz sets entertains during the Southern food dinners, and you can count on a sausage-and-grits gospel brunch on weekends.
✉ **656 125th St at St Clair Pl** ☎ **663-7980** **e** **www.cottonclub-newyork.com** Ⓔ **125th St (1, 9)** 🚌 **M4, M5, M104** ⊘ **Mon-Fri usually from 8pm, Sat-Sun from noon** ⑤ **$15-32**

Danny's Skylight Room (2, N4)
Located behind Danny's Grand Sea Palace (a nice Thai restaurant), this casual cabaret spot lets you get close to performers like Blossom Dearie. Dinner-and-show packages are available.
✉ **346 W 46th St btw 8th & 9th Aves** ☎ **265-8133** **e** **www.dannysgrandseapalace.com** Ⓔ **42nd St-Port Authority** ⊘ **shows 9pm-1am (earlier shows Fri-Sun)** ⑤ **free-$25**

Duplex Cabaret Theatre (3, F4)
Expect cabaret, comedy or small-ensemble performances with mainly gay themes or a campy slant. There's a nightly open mic in the downstairs piano bar – if the customers don't ham it up, the bar staff do. The crowd can sing along – all the better when Broadway singers drop in.
✉ **61 Christopher St at 7th Ave** ☎ **255-5438** Ⓔ **Christopher St-Sheridan Sq** ⊘ **4pm-4am; shows Mon-Sat from 8pm, Sun 7pm** ⑤ **$7-20 & 2-drink minimum**

Ellen's Stardust Diner (2, M5)
It's not just a diner, it's a linoleum-floored cabaret joint starring waiters who can hold a note just as well as they can hold a 'Big Bopper Burger' or a 'Hot Diggity Dog.' Would you like a tune with those fries?
✉ **1650 Broadway at 51st St** ☎ **956-5151, Telecharge 239-6200** **e** **www.ellenstardust.com** Ⓔ **50th St (1, 9)** ⊘ **7am-midnight (Fri-Sat to 1am)** ⑤ **free** ⚿

Feinstein's (2, K7)
Vocalist Michael Feinstein books performers like Rosemary Clooney and Tony Danza to ham it up for the high-rollers at this expensive cabaret club.
✉ **Regency Hotel, 540 Park Ave at 61st St** ☎ **339-4095** **e** **www.feinsteinsattheregency.com** Ⓔ **Lexington Ave (N, R), 59th St (4, 5, 6)** ⑤ **$25-60 & food minimum**

Oak Room at the Algonquin (2, N5)
From in set to twin set, patrons come to soak in the old-money atmosphere at the city's classiest cabaret – a clubby, oak-paneled venue that draws top names and quality newcomers.
✉ **59 W 44th St at 6th Ave** ☎ **840-6800** Ⓔ **42nd St-Grand Central** ⊘ **Tues-Sat dinner from 7:15pm; shows 9pm (also 11pm Fri-Sat)** ⑤ **$15-50**

The Supper Club (2, N4)
Come here for classic New York glam. Dinnertime big-band bashing and cabaret-style revues give way to high-class swing around the witching hour. Dancing lessons are available Saturday at 11:15pm ($5). As the name suggests, you can eat your dinner here. Jackets required; no jeans or sneakers.
✉ **240 W 47th St at Broadway** ☎ **921-1940** **e** **www.thesupperclub.com** Ⓔ **50th St (1, 9), 49th St (N, R)** ⊘ **Fri-Sat 5:30pm-4am** ⑤ **$25 before 11pm, $15 after 11pm**

Flying Solo
New York's not a bad town to be alone in – there's no stigma attached to eating or drinking with a paperback for company. There are even advantages: you can eat at the bar while larger parties wait for restaurant tables, and you can often pick up prime tickets for theater and sporting events simply because you can fit in anywhere. Bars where you'll feel comfortable include **The Scratcher** (p. 96). **Filter 14** (p. 95) is the easiest club to turn up alone at, and **55 Bar** (p. 90) is the nicest jazz-for-one spot.

CLUBS

Centro-Fly (3, D4)

The big and cool Centro-Fly draws lots of island groovers mid-week and mainstream dance bunnies on weekends.

✉ 45 W 21st St btw 5th & 6th Aves ☎ 627-7770 ℮ www.centro-fly.com Ⓜ 23rd St (1, 9, F) ⏰ Wed-Sat 10pm-5:30am Ⓢ $10-25

Filter 14 (3, E2)

Manhattan's friendliest club attracts a mixed crowd ready to dance. The bar staff go at it nearly as hard as the guests. Tuesday and Saturday are the big party nights; Thursday means '80s music.

✉ 432 W 14th St at Washington St ☎ 366-5680 Ⓜ 14th St-8th Ave ⏰ Mon-Wed 8pm-4am, Thurs-Sat 10pm-4am Ⓢ $5-15

Nell's (3, E3)

A well-dressed downtown crowd turns out at this velvet lounge for open mic on Tuesday, 'Latin Night' on Wednesday and karaoke on Sunday. On weekends, a posse of DJs and live bands makes sure everyone's booty is bopping. No sneakers, boots or baggy jeans.

✉ 246 W 14th St btw 7th & 8th Aves ☎ 675-1567 ℮ www.nells.com Ⓜ 14th St-8th Ave ⏰ 10pm-4am Ⓢ $5-10

Shine (3, J5)

This energetic club hosts diverse events. Thursday's 'Giant Step' features hip-hop, funk and soul; Friday means feel-good garage. Other nights, groove to reggae, Bollywood beats and live shows by bands like Fun Lovin' Criminals and Sugar Hill Gang.

✉ 285 W Broadway at Canal St ☎ 941-0900 ℮ www.shinelive.com Ⓜ Canal St (A, C, E) ⏰ varies Ⓢ $5-20

Speeed (2, O6)

Different nights run the gamut from salsa to hip-hop (Saturday) to tribal and back to merengue. Parties for Latin gay porn stars happen regularly.

✉ 20 W 39th St btw 5th & 6th Aves ☎ 719-9867 ℮ www.speeed.com Ⓜ 42nd St, 5th Ave (7) ⏰ Thurs-Sun 10pm-4am Ⓢ varies

Tunnel (3, C1)

Count on a range of house, techno and groovy classics at this massive three-floor club with different DJs on each level. Beware the suburban crowd on weekends.

✉ 220 12th Ave at 27th St ☎ 695-4682 Ⓜ 23rd St (C, E) ⏰ Fri-Sat 10pm-8am Ⓢ around $20

Vinyl (3, K4)

A mixed older crowd comes to this party club where the emphasis is on grooving out rather than seeing-and-being-seen. A sparkling lineup of DJs spins a tasteful mix of funky, classic house and old-time soul. Note: no alcohol.

✉ 6 Hubert St btw Hudson & Greenwich Sts ☎ 343-1379 Ⓜ Franklin St ⏰ Wed 10pm-4am, Fri-Sat 11pm-late, Sun 4pm-late Ⓢ $14-20

How to Get into Club Fab

The easiest way to slip into of-the-moment clubs is to be famous, fabulous and friends with the scenesters – ie, it's not always easy. But there are other ways of getting on the guest list. Look for flyers, posters and ads with phone numbers and email addresses for club nights, then get in touch with promoters ahead of time to request a spot on the list. It doesn't always mean free entry, but it at least means you get in. Some clubs keep email lists and send out passwords each week.

Party till the wee hours.

Jeff Greenberg

BARS & LOUNGES

Beauty Bar (3, E7)
Haven't you always wanted to sip on a cocktail while sitting under an old hair-drying cone? Sure ya have. This bar, inside a not-quite-converted old beauty salon, comes complete with DJs, live music and beautician. 'Truckstop Tuesday' features tear-jerkin' road anthems.
✉ 231 E 14th St btw 2nd & 3rd Aves ☎ 539-1389 🚇 3rd Ave
🚌 M14 ⏰ 5pm-4am

Belmont Lounge
(3, E6) This hip, snappy and spacious spot has lots of nooks for those with serious gossip or an eye to romance. Stargazers should head to the garden. You

can order food at all hours to fortify yourself. DJs spin on weekends.
✉ 117 E 15th St at Irving Pl ☎ 533-0009
🚇 Union Sq ⏰ noon-4am ⓢ free-$5

Bowlmor Lanes (3, E5)
Bowling, drinks and disco – everything is fun when you're wearing two-tone shoes. Come Monday night for glow-in-the-dark techno bowling. Games are cheapest before 5pm. Kids, though welcome, have to clear out by 6pm.
✉ 110 University Pl btw 12th & 13th Sts
☎ 255-8188
✉ www.bowlmor.com
🚇 Union Sq ⏰ Mon &

Fri 10am-4am, Tues-Wed 10am-1am, Thurs 10am-2am, Sat 11am-4am, Sun 11am-1am ⓢ under $10 ♿

Cabana (3, M7)
Definitely the coolest bar on the Pier, Cabana serves Nuevo Latino bar snacks like plantain chips and conch fritters with your ice-cold Corona. If you sit on the deck and look south, Lady Liberty appears to be joining in the toast.
✉ 3rd fl, 89 South St ☎ 406-1155 ✉ www .southstreetseaport.com 🚇 Fulton St 🚌 M15 ⏰ 11am-midnight (Fri-Sat to 1am); closes earlier in winter

Pub Crawl
One beer, hold the attitude? Stop in at one of these welcoming Manhattan pubs.

Chumley's (86 Bedford St btw Grove & Barrow Sts; 3, G4; ☎ 675-4449; ⏰ 4pm-2am), a sawdust-on-the-floor, jocks-at-the-bar kind of place, serves decent pub grub and microbrews.

At the friendly **Ear Inn** (326 Spring St btw Greenwich & Washington Sts; 3, J4; ☎ 226-9060; ⏰ bar 11am-4am, kitchen closes earlier), in an old Federal house, Tuesday is bikers' evening, and Saturday is poetry afternoon; every night is Guinness night.

The amiable crowd'll talk baseball or philosophy at the popular **Kinsale Tavern** (1672 3rd Ave at E 93rd St; 2, D7; ☎ 348-4370; ⏰ Mon-Thurs 8am-1:30am, Fri-Sat 8am-3:30am), where you can choose from 20 beers on tap.

The Scratcher (209 E 5th St btw 2nd & 3rd Aves; 3, G6; ☎ 477-0030; ⏰ 11:30am-4am) is a true Dublin-style pub: a quiet place to read the newspaper during the day over coffee but a crowded and raucous spot at night.

Kim Grant

Cafe St Barts (2, M7)

The big outdoor terrace next to St Bartholomew's Church offers eats and drinks and occasional live jazz. The 'holy cow!' location should keep you on the narrow, if not exactly the straight. The church is open till 6pm for 'quiet contemplation.'

✉ 109 E 50th St at Park Ave ☎ 888-2664 🚇 51st St, Lexington Ave (E, F) 🚌 M50 🕐 Mon-Sat noon-11pm, Sun noon-4pm ♿

The Campbell Apartment (2, N6)

Built by tycoon John Campbell as a 1920s hideaway, this Italian villa–like apartment was later used as a police depot and signal room. Now it's a discreet bar with heaps of class, a serious dress code (you can't wear sneakers or T-shirts) and simply brilliant cocktails.

✉ 15 Vanderbilt Ave btw 42nd & 43rd Sts, in Grand Central Terminal ☎ 953-0409 e www .grandcentralterminal .com 🚇 42nd St-Grand Central 🕐 Mon-Sat 3pm-1am, Sun 3-11pm

Chez es Saada (3, G7)

Stay upstairs in the bar/bistro or tread the rose-petal-strewn staircase to the cellarish lounge. Eat modern Moroccan fare or juice up on frou-frou cocktails and make goo-goo eyes at tomorrow's supermodels. Belly dancers perform on Friday and Saturday.

✉ 42 E 1st St btw 1st & 2nd Aves ☎ 777-5617 🚇 2nd Ave 🕐 Sun-Wed 6pm-midnight, Thurs-Sat 6pm-2am

Cafe St Barts

Angus Oborn

Double Happiness (3, J6)

Go early so you can grab a table in this dank, underground ex-speakeasy with an obscure entrance – look for 'watch your step' and a stairway down. Sunday features make-out parties.

✉ 173 Mott St btw Broome & Grand Sts ☎ 941-1282 🚇 Spring St (6), Bowery 🕐 6pm-4am

The Evelyn Lounge (2, G4)

This clubby, multi-room cellar features a classy cigar lounge and a martini list with more options than the light 'n' fresh dinner menu. The laid-back crowd that comes during the week makes room for hobnobbing students on the weekend.

✉ 380 Columbus Ave at W 78th St ☎ 724-2363 e www.evelyn-lounge.com 🚇 81st St 🚌 M79 🕐 6pm-4am

Lakeside Lounge (3, F8)

Come to this slightly grungy, firmly casual hangout for free bands, cheap drinks and a black-and-white-photo booth – you need only $3

to remember the night forever.

✉ 162 Ave B at E 10th St ☎ 529-8463 🚇 1st Ave 🚌 M9, M14 🕐 4pm-4am

Liquor Store (3, K5)

A local hangout with big street-watching windows, this friendly corner bar draws crowds of interlopers toward the weekend. You'll find plenty of people to talk to and outdoor tables when the weather is kind.

✉ 235 W Broadway at White St ☎ 226-7121 🚇 Franklin St 🕐 noon-4am

Open (3, D2)

This airy bar is a cruisy 'tween-gallery hangout during the day (sandwiches and cookies available), but by the time the sun's setting over the Hudson, it's hopping with the post-gym Chelsea Piers crowd and other incoming wounded. Snacks fortify the workout-depleted till late.

✉ 559 W 22nd St at 11th Ave ☎ 243-1851 🚇 23rd St (C, E) 🚌 M23 🕐 noon-4am

Rainbow by Cipriani (2, M6)

Cocktails are $16, so it's lucky that there's a million-dollar view. Take dinner in the restaurant or nosh on $4 bar sandwiches and chat with the veteran bartenders. The grand Rainbow Room, open to the public once a week, features prix fixe dinners ($110) and a rotating dance floor.

✉ 65th fl, 30 Rockefeller Plaza at 49th St ☎ 632-5100 e www.cipriani.com 🚇 Rockefeller Center 🕐 noon-1am

GAY & LESBIAN NEW YORK

Time Out New York and the *Village Voice* have special listings for gay party-hunters. *Blade*, *Homo Xtra*, *LGNY* and *Next* are free gay newspapers that are available in city bars, clubs and bookshops. Also check out the websites [e] www.nyblade.com and [e] www.hx.com for listings. For more information, see Gay & Lesbian Travelers (p. 120).

B Bar (3, G6)

A big bar/restaurant with a high beautiful-person factor, B Bar gets busy most nights. Tuesday draws a high-energy mixed crowd. Celebrities from the fashion and movie-making worlds have been known to drop by. The garden stays open in winter.

✉ 40 E 4th St at Bowery ☎ 475-2220 [e] www.bbar.citysearch .com 🚇 2nd Ave ⏰ 11:30am-4am (Sat-Sun from 10:30am)

The Cock (3, F8)

DJs, dancing and drag make for a wild Saturday night through-the-roof party at this boozy, cruisy club. The crowd is old-school East Village: unpretentious and arty, with the odd leather-dressed go-go boy thrown in.

✉ 188 Ave A at 12th St ☎ 777-6254 🚇 1st Ave 🚌 M14 ⏰ 9:30pm-4am 💲 around $2

Crazy Nanny's (3, G4)

This brash bar for gay women and their friends features a Monday pool tournament, Wednesday and Sunday karaoke, classic drag on Thursday and exotic dancers on Friday and Saturday. It can get crowded and raucous on weekends.

✉ 21 7th Ave S at Leroy St ☎ 366-6312 [e] www.crazynannys .com 🚇 Houston St ⏰ Mon-Fri 4pm-4am, Sat-Sun 3pm-4am 💲 free during week, $8-15 Thurs-Sat

Don Hill's (3, J4)

Lesbian rock, transvestite pole dancers and porn projections on the walls mix with soul, Brit pop and straight-ahead dance music at this varied gay/straight nightspot.

✉ 511 Greenwich St at Spring St ☎ 334-1390 🚇 Spring St (C, E) ⏰ 10pm-4am

Hell (3, F3)

Despite the forbidding name, the feeling is friendly at this smallish lounge with luscious red drapery and cutesy photos of celebs with devilish horns. The mixed crowd tends to be laid-back. Sunday is disco night.

✉ 59 Gansevoort St btw Greenwich & Hudson Sts ☎ 727-1666 🚇 14th St-8th Ave ⏰ 7pm-4am (Sat-Sun from 5pm) 💲 varies

Henrietta Hudson

(3, H4) This dive bar for women makes a good meeting place or an easy spot to sit and feel comfortably unhassled with a brewski. You can also play pool or listen to the DJs and occasional live music.

✉ 438 Hudson St at Morton St ☎ 924-3347 🚇 Houston St ⏰ 4pm-4am (Sat-Sun from 1pm)

Heaven (3, E4)

Though the halo promises an angelic vibe, the college boys and go-go dancers get just plain naughty on three floors, which have been zoned purgatory, heaven and hell. Be as dancey or loungey, good or bad as you like.

✉ 579 6th Ave btw 16th & 17th Sts ☎ 243-6100 🚇 6th Ave, 14th St (F) ⏰ 5pm-4am 💲 $5-15

The Stonewall Rebellion

On June 27, 1969, the Stonewall Inn, a men's bar filled with patrons mourning the death of Judy Garland, was raided by the police. A spirited resistance by patrons escalated into three nights of riots, galvanizing the gay rights movement and conferring sacred-site status on Christopher St at Sheridan Square (later renamed Stonewall Place). The Pride March (late June) pays homage to the site every year. Today's **Stonewall Inn** (53 Christopher St; 3, G4); ☎ 463-0950), though a gay bar, is not the original.

Lure (3, E3)

Dress leather, denim or uniform at this popular leather and fetish bar with an exclusively gay crowd and a strictly enforced dress code. Monday is foot fetish night, and Wednesday might include body painting, piercing or pornographic performances.
✉ 409 W 13th St at 9th Ave ☎ 741-3919 Ⓜ 14th St-8th Ave ⏰ Mon-Sat 8pm-4am, Sun noon-4am

Marie's Crisis (3, G4)

In business for more than 30 years, this wonderful tavern caters mostly to older gays. The show tunes often involve everyone in the place gathering around the piano and joining in for the chorus.
✉ 59 Grove St at 7th Ave ☎ 243-9323 Ⓜ Christopher St-Sheridan Sq ⏰ 4pm-4am

Meow Mix (3, G8)

It's not big, but this lesbian club packs a purr with a lively lineup of bands, DJs and saucy performances. You can also just prop yourself at the bar for some chatting and checking out the scene.
✉ 269 E Houston at Suffolk St ☎ 254-0688 e www.meowmixchix .com Ⓜ Delancey-Essex Sts ⏰ Mon 7pm-4am, Tues-Fri 5pm-4am, Sat-Sun 3pm-4am ⓢ around $5

The Monster (3, G4)

This up-for-anything club includes a piano bar upstairs and a dance floor below (dancing boys perform nightly at 11pm). It's a comfortable place for all ages (over 21) and races.
✉ 80 Grove St at W 4th St ☎ 924-3558 Ⓜ Christopher St-Sheridan Sq ⏰ 4pm-4am (Sat-Sun from 2pm)

Rubyfruit Bar & Grill (3, G3)

An older lesbian contingent and a welcoming regular crowd make this a civilized spot where weekend entertainment runs from piano bar schmaltz to '50s bop.
✉ 531 Hudson St at Charles St ☎ 929-3343 Ⓜ 14th St-8th Ave ⏰ Mon-Sat 3pm-2am (Fri-Sat to 4am), Sun 11:30am-2am

Splash (3, E4)

An upscale crowd frequents this exclusively gay video dance bar with four bar areas and two-for-one happy hours every afternoon. It's not the place for shrinking violets – even the urinals are porny and provocative.
✉ 50 W 17th St at 6th Ave ☎ 691-0073 e www.splashbar.com Ⓜ 6th Ave, 14th St (F) ⏰ 4pm-4am (Fri-Sat to 5am) ⓢ free-$10

B is for beautiful: a young crowd frequents the B Bar.

Angus Oborn

CINEMAS

Angelika Film Center
(3, H6) The Angelika
always draws weekend
crowds for its 'films, not
movies.' It's inside the Old
Cable Building, which used
to house cables for city
trolley cars.
✉ **18 W Houston St at
Mercer St** ☎ **995-
2000, 777-3456 (press
#531)** e **www.city
cinemas.com** Ⓜ **Bleec-
ker St, Broadway-
Lafayette St** 🚇 **M21**

**Anthology Film
Archives** (3, G7)
Film-buff heaven, this spot
shows far-out fringe and

foreign films, works by
local filmmakers and otherwise unreleased fare.
✉ **32 2nd Ave at E 2nd
St** ☎ **505-5110**
e **www.anthology
filmarchives.org**
Ⓜ **2nd Ave**

Cinema Classics (3, F7)
See auteur and cult films
(Altman, Almodovar,
Tarkovsky) on 16mm in a
lounge-like theaterette –
this is a real East Village
bargain. Before the show,
check out the video and
DVD shop and café.
✉ **332 E 11th St btw
1st & 2nd Aves** ☎ **971-**

1015 e **www.cinema
classics.com** Ⓜ **1st
Ave, Astor Pl** Ⓢ **$5.50**

Film Forum (3, H4)
Independent and repertory
films show on three
screens. Themed programs
can be fun and thought-
provoking, like the series
devoted to the city's police
department.
✉ **209 W Houston St
btw 6th Ave & Varick St**
☎ **727-8110** e **www
.filmforum.com**
Ⓜ **Houston St** 🚇 **M21**
Ⓢ **$9**

Screening Room
(3, J5)
Favorites over the Screening
Room's five-year history
include *Willy Wonka* and a
3-D disco-porn movie.
Regular fare isn't always so
out-there, but it's usually
alternative enough to
please the local loft-
dwellers. A good restaurant
onsite offers some prix fixe
dinner-and-movie deals.
✉ **54 Varick St at Canal
St** ☎ **334-2100**
e **www.thescreening
room.com** Ⓜ **Canal St
(1, 9, A, C, E), 3rd Ave**

**Walter Reade
Theater at Lincoln
Center** (2, K3)
Here you can see inde-
pendent films, career retrospectives and themed
series, plus screenings at
the New York Film Festival
every September.
✉ **165 W 65th St btw
Amsterdam &
Broadway, Lincoln
Center** ☎ **875-5600**
e **www.filmlinc.com**
Ⓜ **66th St-Lincoln
Center**

The Small-Screen Scene

Free tickets are available for a number of TV show
tapings. Tickets for many shows are sold months in
advance, but you can often get standby tickets on
the day of taping. **NBC** (☎ 664-3056) distributes
tickets from its premises (30 Rockefeller Plaza, on
49th St; 2, M6). Stand in line for *The Rosie O'Donnell
Show* Monday to Thursday at 7:30am, *Late Night
with Conan O'Brien* Tuesday to Friday at 9am and
Saturday Night Live Saturday at 9:15am. **CBS**
(☎ 247-6497) sometimes offers standby tickets for
The Late Show with David Letterman, taped at the
Ed Sullivan Theater (Broadway at 53rd St; 2, M5); call
the network Monday to Thursday at 11am. If you do
get a ticket, take something warm to wear to the
taping – the studios are freezing.

As seen on TV

Richard I'Anson

SPECTATOR SPORTS

New Yorkers are a sporty lot, though their equipment is more often TV, beer and peanuts than racquets, bats and balls. They fancy themselves the most ardent, knowledgeable and loyal fans anywhere and will happily argue the merits of pitchers, receivers and owners while riding the subway, standing in line for brunch or waiting for the opera to start.

One of the 'Bronx Bombers' (Yankees) steps up to the plate.

The game that became known as **baseball** was first called the 'New York game' when its rules were written down in 1846. Baseball traditions that began in New York include the eating of hot dogs at the game (1900) and the playing of 'Take Me Out to the Ball Game' (1908). The city's pro baseball teams are the extraordinarily successful Yankees (American League), who keep winning the World Series (or coming oh-so-close), and the ugly duckling Mets (National League). The season runs April to October.

The game of **basketball** was invented in Massachusetts, but New York is its heartland. New York's NBA team is the Knicks. There's strong support for the New York Liberty women's team, too. Both of these teams play at Madison Square Garden – expect to see Spike Lee and Woody Allen at Knicks games. The New Jersey Nets, part of the NBA, play at the Meadowlands. The NBA season runs October to May.

New York Giants **football** tickets sell out years in advance; season tickets can be hotly contested in divorce battles and left to children in wills. New York Jets tickets are easier to come by. The NFL season runs September to January.

Babe Ruth

George Herman Ruth (1895–1948) is the most famous Yankee. Known as 'The Babe' or the 'Sultan of Swat,' the left-handed slugger was baseball's first superstar, an icon whose on- and off-field charisma helped make baseball the national pastime. The first to hit three home runs in a game (in the 1926 World Series), Ruth was an early inductee into baseball's Hall of Fame; he starred as himself in the 1942 film *Pride of the Yankees*.

Angus Oborn

The New York Rangers play **ice hockey** at Madison Square Garden October to April. Their rivals, the New York Islanders, play at Nassau Veterans Memorial Coliseum. The New Jersey Devils take to the ice at the Meadowlands.

The US Open is the year's final Grand Slam **tennis** event (with the finals played over the Labor Day weekend); it takes place at the National Tennis Center. Reserved tickets are only required for Arthur Ashe Stadium, which sells out months ahead. Day-session grounds passes are sold on the morning of each day's play – if you're in line before 9am, you might snag one.

Belmont Park is the area's biggest horse-racing track. The season runs May to July.

You can purchase tickets for most big sporting events through Ticketmaster (☎ 307-7171).

Sporting Venues

Belmont Park (Hempstead Turnpike, Elmont, Long Island; ☎ 516-488-6000; 🄴 www.nyra.com; 🄶 LIRR from Penn Station to Belmont) – horse racing; Belmont Stakes race in June

Madison Square Garden (8th Ave at W 33rd St; 2, P4; ☎ 465-6741; 🄴 www .thegarden.com; 🄶 Penn Station) – basketball, hockey

Meadowlands Sports Complex (East Rutherford, New Jersey; 4, B1; ☎ 201-935-3900; 🄴 www.meadowlands.com) – New York Giants and Jets football, New Jersey Nets basketball, New Jersey Devils hockey

Nassau Veterans Memorial Coliseum (1255 Hempstead Turnpike, Uniondale, Long Island; ☎ 516-794-9300; 🄴 www.nassaucoliseum.com; 🄶 LIRR to Hempstead, then bus N70-72) – ice hockey and New York Saints indoor lacrosse

National Tennis Center (Flushing Meadows-Corona Park, Queens; 6, B4; ☎ 718-760-6200, tickets 866-673-6849; 🄴 www.usopen.org; 🄶 Shea Stadium-Willets Point) – tennis

Shea Stadium (Flushing Meadows, Queens; 6, B4; ☎ 718-507-8499, tickets 718-507-8499; 🄴 www.mets.com; 🄶 Shea Stadium-Willets Point; NY Waterway ferry from South Street Seaport) – New York Mets baseball

Yankee Stadium (161st St at River Ave, the Bronx; 4, A2; ☎ 718-293-6000; 🄴 www.yankees.com; 🄶 161st St-Yankee Stadium; New York Waterway ferry from South Street Seaport) – New York Yankees baseball

The 'house that Ruth built': Yankee Stadium

places to stay

Need a place to rest your head? Your options include some of the grandest hotels in the world, hip boutique hotels, anonymous but bustling mid-price places, cozy private guesthouses and cheaper lodges. But New York suffers from a desperate shortage of reasonably priced places to stay – rooms under $80 a night are usually only found in dives or shared-room hostels.

Accommodations in New York are tight all year long. If you can, book well in advance and confirm

Room Rates

These price ranges indicate the walk-up rates for one night in a standard double room.

Top End	from $300
Mid-Range	$120-299
Budget	under $120

Booking Agencies

Booking agencies reserve rooms in bulk, supposedly giving them the buying power to pass on large discounts. The mid-range hotel rates they offer usually don't drop much below the rack rate, though the agencies do a better job with higher cost accommodations.

- **Budget Hotel Finders** (☎ 516-771-7213, 800-382-7213; [e] www.bookahotel.com)
- **Central Reservations Service** (☎ 407-740-6442, 800-555-7555; [e] www.reservation services.com)
- **Express Reservations** (☎ 303-440-8481, 800-407-3351; [e] www.express-res.com)
- **Hotel Discounts** (☎ 800-715-7666; [e] www.hoteldiscounts.com)

your arrival date with the hotel a week before you intend to arrive. When booking, ask about reduced weekend rates and other packages that can include upgraded rooms, complimentary meals and car service. Be sure to allow for taxes, which add a hefty slug to your bill and are rarely included in quoted room rates. You'll pay 13.25% in city and state taxes, as well as a $2 occupancy tax for each normal-size room.

If you're traveling to New York on a sudden impulse, or that friend of a friend with a spare bed in a Soho loft suddenly gets a visit from his parents, get on the phone or the Internet right away. A last-minute bed hunt is more likely to lead to dead ends than cheap standby room rates, though you could be lucky.

A posh place to lay your head: Peninsula

TOP END

If money grows on your trees, you won't do better than New York's finest hotels. Expect impeccable service, excellent climate control, 24-hour room service, premium cable TV, data ports, a fax machine and a large tub.

Four Seasons (2, L6)
This IM Pei/Frank Williams–designed limestone monolith is the tallest hotel in New York (52 floors) and boasts the largest rooms. Children get balloons and milk and cookies on arrival. It's arty (note the Magritte and Kandinsky), and the public spaces are epic.
✉ **57 E 57th St btw Park & Madison Aves** ☎ **758-5700 fax 758-5711** e **www.fourseasons.com** ⊖ **5th Ave (N, R), 59th St (4, 5, 6)** ✕ **Fifty Seven Fifty Seven Restaurant & Bar, Lobby Lounge** ⚲

Library Hotel (2, O6)
Each room in this charming hotel is dedicated to a different genre of books. Dotcommers gravitate to the Technology floor, literati choose between Classics and Fiction rooms, while honeymooners zoom for the Erotic. Continental breakfast and evening hors d'oeuvres are complimentary.
✉ **299 Madison Ave at 41st St** ☎ **983-4500,** 877-793-7323 fax 499-9099 e **www.libraryhotel.com** ⊖ **42nd St-Grand Central** ✕ **Vigneti** ⚲

The Michelangelo (2, M5) An escape from anonymous chains, this hotel is owned by an Italian family with an eye for guest comfort. The rooms are so spacious you could bathe a pony in the tub. For business types, there's complimentary shoeshine and limousine service to Wall St.
✉ **152 W 51st St at 7th Ave** ☎ **765-0505 fax 581-7618** e **www.michelangelohotel.com** ⊖ **50th St (1, 9), 49th St** ✕ **Limoncello** ⚲

New York Palace (2, M6) Large rooms feature great views, capacious beds, high-quality linens and bathrooms that make getting dirty worthwhile. Those staying in the Tower Suites enjoy access to separate check-in counters and elevators, plus butlers on every floor. The famous,

Indulge at a top spot.

somewhat overrated Le Cirque 2000 restaurant is here if you care to splurge.
✉ **455 Madison Ave at 50th St** ☎ **888-7000,** 800-697-2522 fax 303-6000 e **www.newyorkpalace.com** ⊖ **51st (6), Lexington Ave (E, F)** ✕ **Le Cirque 2000, Istana** ⚲

Parker-Meridien (2, L5) A matter-of-fact eliteness pervades this hotel, from the so-low-key-it's-almost-secret lobby to the 'fuhgeddaboudit' Do Not Disturb signs. Suitedwellers can savor the Central Park view. Tennis players and officials stay here during the US Open, partly because of the well-equipped fitness center and large pool with a view.
✉ **118 W 57th St btw 6th & 7th Aves** ☎ **245-5000 fax 307-1776** e **www.parkermeridien.com** ⊖ **57th St (B, Q, N, R)** ✕ **Norma's, Seppi's** ⚲

Short-Term Apartments

A well-established B&B agency, **At Home In New York** (☎ 956-3125; e athomeny@erols.com) rents out about 300 guestrooms all over Manhattan.

A Hospitality Company (☎ 965-1102, 800-987-1235; fax 965-1149; e www.hospitalityco.com) rents apartments ranging from studios to two-bedrooms sleeping six people. Nightly rates with both agencies are comparable to those charged by the cheapest hotels; weekly rates are available.

Peninsula (2, L6)
Gorgeous art nouveau rooms feature one-touch mood lighting, in-room temperature display and a privacy button to deactivate your doorbell. The pool is almost big enough for laps, and the Pen-Top bar is tops among sunset-watching Manhattanites.
✉ **700 5th Ave at 55th St** ☎ **956-2888 fax 903-3949** ℮ **www .peninsula.com** Ⓜ **57th St (B, Q)** ✗ **Adrienne, Pen-Top Bar, Gotham Lounge & Bistro** ♿

The Pierre (2, K6)
The only trouble with The Pierre is that it's so nice you'll have a hard time leaving your room – no one's going to be this friendly and attentive once you hit the street. If you do get outside, you'll love the location: between Central Park and Madison Ave's top shops.
✉ **5th Ave at 61st St** ☎ **838-8000, 800-743-7734 fax 826-0319** ℮ **www.fourseasons .com** Ⓜ **5th Ave (N, R)** ✗ **The Rotunda, Cafe Pierre**

The Regent Wall Street (3, N6)
This grand Greek Revival building (1842) served as New York's stock exchange and customs house. Today, it features a massive ballroom with a domed Wedgwood ceiling. The 144 rooms are spacious and classically furnished, with oversized tubs and TVs.
✉ **55 Wall St at William St** ☎ **845-8600 fax 845-8601** ℮ **www .regenthotels.com** Ⓜ **Wall St, Rector St** ✗ **55 Wall**

Traveling with Children
Most hotels welcome children and will set up cots in guestrooms at no extra charge. The fancier hotels offer extras like special room-service menus, video games and toys. Check the cutoff age for such privileges when reserving your room. A surprising number of New York hotels also welcome kids of the four-legged variety – see the **Soho Grand Hotel** (below).

---

60 Thompson St
(3, J5) This discreet Soho pad includes just over 100 stylish rooms in muted earth colors with DVDs and marble bathrooms. The rooms are good for entertaining, but take a suite if you're working – otherwise your laptop really will be on your lap. Check out the rooftop garden.
✉ **60 Thompson St btw Broome & Spring Sts** ☎ **431-0400, 877-431-0400 fax 431-0200** ℮ **www.60thompson .com** Ⓜ **Canal St (A, C, E)** ✗ **Thom**

Soho Grand Hotel
(3, K5) The industrial chic entrance – all buffed metal – sets the scene. This comfort zone for the young and splashy prides itself on being pet-friendly. Your pooch can sleep in your room, and the hotel will even supply the petless with a goldfish that you can take home with you.
✉ **310 W Broadway at Canal St** ☎ **965-3000 fax 965-3200** ℮ **www .sohogrand.com** Ⓜ **Canal St (A, C, E)** ✗ **Canal House** ♿

St Regis (2, L6)
This gorgeous beaux arts building in the heart of the city offers large, comfy rooms and impeccable, discreet service. The King Cole bar downstairs lays claim to inventing the Bloody Mary.
✉ **2 E 55th St at 5th Ave** ☎ **753-4500, 800-759-7550 fax 787-3447** ℮ **www.stregis.com** Ⓜ **57th St (B, Q)** ✗ **Lespinasse** ♿

Waldorf-Astoria
(2, M7) This art deco treasure is showing some wear and tear, so it's cheaper than Midtown's other big-name hotels. Pleasant rooms, some recently renovated, feature comfortable beds and spacious bathrooms – though some can be dim.
✉ **301 Park Ave at 50th St** ☎ **355-3000, 800-925-3673 fax 872-7272** ℮ **www.waldorf astoria.com** Ⓜ **51st St, Lexington Ave (E, F)** ✗ **Oscar's, Inagiku, Bull & Bear, Peacock Alley** ♿

Michelle Bennett

Waldorf-Astoria: where the salad began

MID-RANGE

Most of Manhattan's hotels fall into this price range. Expect private bathrooms (usually with a bathtub), sizable closets, air-conditioning, voicemail and often a fax machine.

Ameritania (2, L4)
A sleek lobby and stylish (but small) rooms distinguish this spot, which enjoys a Broadway location. Rooms of the same price vary a lot in size – request a larger, street-facing room when booking.
✉ **230 W 54th St at Broadway** ☎ **247-5000 fax 247-3313** |e| **www .nycityhotels.net** Ⓜ **7th Ave** ✗ **Twist** ⚡

Clarion Hotel (2, O6)
Aimed at leisure travelers, families and budgeting business folk, this place has all the facilities but none of the flash. The location is great, the kids-free policy enticing and the rooms workable.
✉ **3 E 40th at 5th Ave** ☎ **447-1500 fax 685-5214** |e| **www.clarion hotel.com** Ⓜ **42nd St-Grand Central** ⚡

The Franklin (2, F7)
After elbowing through the tiny lobby, you'll be

Park included: Gramercy Park Hotel

Michelle Bennett

pleased to note you can almost swing a cat in the Franklin's pleasant rooms. Cotton linens make the beds comfortable, and Aveda products make the bathroom classy. The location is great – a quick walk from Museum Mile and seconds from the subway.
✉ **164 E 87th St at Lexington Ave** ☎ **369-1000 fax 369-8000** |e| **www.franklinhotel .com** Ⓜ **86th St (4, 5, 6)**

Gramercy Park Hotel (3, D6) Not as charming as it claims to be, this comfortable old favorite with just over 500 rooms does have more character than the city's bland newer hotels. Guests enjoy access to the locked, lovely Gramercy Park and the Gothic National Arts Club mansion.
✉ **2 Lexington Ave at 21st St** ☎ **475-4320 fax 505-0535** |e| **www .gramercyparkhotel.com** ✗ **Le Parc** ⚡

Holiday Inn (3, J6)
Location and price (not the small rooms) are the draw cards at this chain hotel with no surprises. You're in the middle of Chinatown and an easy walk away from Lower Manhattan, Soho and Tribeca. Faxes are provided in suites only.
✉ **138 Lafayette St at Canal St** ☎ **966-8898 fax 966-3933** |e| **www. holiday-inn.com/hotels /nycdt** Ⓜ **Canal St (N, R, S, 6)** ✗ **Pacifica** ⚡

Hotel Gershwin (3, C5)
NYC dream: you enter a red-and-black stylin' lobby, line up with the groove train for the sloooow elevator (ignoring the Warhol-signed soup can on the wall). You enter a spacious room with pop furniture, freshen up in your jaunty bathroom and watch TV from the bed without wrenching your neck. Doze off. Wake up. Pinch yourself. It was no dream.
✉ **7 E 27th St btw 5th & Madison Aves** ☎ **545-8000 fax 684-5546** |e| **www .gershwinhotel.com** Ⓜ **28th St (N, R)** ✗ **Gershwin Cafe** ⚡

Hudson (2, L4)
This Ian Schrager–owned, Philippe Starck–designed 1000-roomer slurps up in-crowd aspirants via a glowing tube escalator to the almost-too-happening lobby. Check out the funkarama chandelier and the fancy Hudson Bar. Rooms are a tad small but well decked out, the cheapest under $100.
✉ **356 W 58th St at 9th Ave** ☎ **554-6000 fax 554-6001** Ⓜ **Columbus Circle** ✗ **Hudson Cafeteria**

The Lucerne (2, G3)
Hard to beat in the neighborhood, this hotel has location, comfort and value all sewn up. Try to snag a street-facing room for more light and better views – the corner suites aren't

much pricier than the deluxe rooms.
✉ **201 W 79th St at Amsterdam Ave** ☎ **875-1000, 800-492-8122 fax 721-1179** e **www.newyorkhotel.com** 🅜 **79th St** ✕ **Wilson's** ♿

Off Soho Suites

(3, H7) Close to Soho, this place offers an excellent value for families or groups – the suites are clean without being fancy, sleep up to four in two rooms and feature a good-size bathroom and functional kitchen. Going cheaper means you share bathroom and kitchen with one other room.
✉ **11 Rivington St at Bowery** ☎ **979-9808, 800-633-7646 fax 979-9801** e **www.offsoho.com** 🅜 **Broadway-Lafayette St, Spring St (6)** ✕ **Off Soho Suites Cafe** ♿

On The Ave

(2, G3) Well-lit rooms feature clever fittings such as stainless steel sinks. The superior rooms don't win in the size category; they're just a little more ornate.
✉ **2178 Broadway at W 77th St** ☎ **362-1100, 800-497-6028 fax 787-9521** e **www.ontheave-nyc.com** 🅜 **79th St**

The Time

(2, M4) Frequented by the young and snappy, this newish hotel offers small but stylish rooms decked out in solid primary colors (check with your aura therapist before you reserve). Bose sound systems, ergonomic work stations and impeccable bathrooms (most with shower only) raise the bar

Art gallery meets hotel at the Gershwin.

Angus Oborn

for the around $200 mark.
✉ **224 W 49th St btw Broadway & 8th Ave** ☎ **246-5252 fax 245-2305** e **www.thetimeny.com** 🅜 **50th St (1, 9)** ✕ **Coco Pazza Teatro** ♿

Washington Square Hotel

(3, F5) This friendly hotel with cramped rooms rides on its great location and its history (Bob Dylan lived here for a while). If you just need to flop after a day of mooching around the Village, this hotel will suit fine.
✉ **103 Waverly Pl btw 5th & 6th Aves** ☎ **777-9515 fax 979-8373** e **www.wshotel.com** 🅜 **W 4th St** ✕ **C3 Restaurant & Bar**

Union Square Inn

(3, E7) If 'hotel' just means 'crash pad' to you, then this cramped five-floor walk-up

should suit. The rooms in this new hotel are clean and air-conditioned but very small. The location and price, though, are great.
✉ **209 E 14th St btw Ave A & 1st Ave** ☎ **614-0500 fax 614-0512** e **www.unionsquareinn.com** 🅜 **1st Ave** ♿

YMCA Vanderbilt

(2, N8) This clean, well-run Y offers private rooms with TV and air-con, some of which have bathrooms. It's in a quiet part of Midtown, near the UN but an easy walk to Grand Central Terminal and the shopping district on 5th Ave.
✉ **224 E 47th St btw 2nd & 3rd Aves** ☎ **756-9600 fax 752-0210** e **www.ymcanyc.org** 🅜 **42nd St-Grand Central** 🚌 **M15, M27, M50** ✕ **International Cafe** ♿

Gay & Lesbian Accommodations

You're unlikely to find any hotel in New York blinking an eyelid at same-sex couples sharing, though some tend to be more welcoming than others. The **Washington Square Hotel** (above) and the **Gramercy Park Hotel** (p. 106) are gay-friendly. The **Colonial House Inn** (318 W 22nd St at 8th Ave; 3, D3; ☎ 243-9669) and the **Chelsea Pines Inn** (317 W 14th St at 8th Ave; 3, E3; ☎ 929-1023) are popular with gay men. The celeb-drawing **Mercer Hotel** (99 Prince St at Mercer St; 3, H5; ☎ 966-6060) welcomes guests in any configuration.

BUDGET

People may begin giggling when you ask about budget accommodations in New York – it is largely a laughable concept. The places listed here offer reasonable, if not luxurious, facilities, and most are shared-bath affairs.

Alladin Hotel (2, N4)

Close to Times Square, this hostel contains single-sex and coed dorms with three to 12 beds (from $35). Private rooms start at $75. All share bathrooms. It's a young, friendly, slightly chaotic place.
✉ 317 W 45th St btw 8th & 9th Aves ☎ 246-8580 fax 246-6036 e www.alladinhotel .com 🚇 42nd St-Port Authority

Cosmopolitan Hotel

(3, L5) Convenient to the financial district and Tribeca's restaurants and bars, this budget hotel offers clean, cramped rooms. The cheapest are dog houses with loft beds, but don't think claustrophobic, think authentic – even quintessential – New York pad.
✉ 95 W Broadway at Chambers St ☎ 566-1900, 888-895-9400 fax 566-6909 e www .cosmohotel.com 🚇 Chambers St

Herald Square Hotel

(3, B5) Built in the 1890s to house *Life* magazine, this hotel has hung onto its past: the golden cherub who graced the cover of the magazine still sits above the doorway. These days, the babe oversees low prices, good rooms and a constant stream of guests. Family rooms are a good deal.
✉ 19 W 31st St btw 5th Ave & Broadway

☎ 279-4017, 800-727-1888 fax 643-9208 e www.heraldsquare hotel.com 🚇 33rd St, Herald Sq

Hotel Grand Union

(3, B5) Family or quad rooms are a good value for the money at this spot, where the newly refurbished, fairly spacious rooms boast a comfortable feel and cable TV. But this is not the place to come if you want to be coddled – the staff don't put on any airs but are nevertheless efficient.
✉ 34 E 32nd St btw Madison & Park Aves ☎ 683-5890 fax 689-7397 e www.hotel grandunion.com 🚇 33rd St 🍴 Tony's Burger

Hotel 17 (3, E7)

This slightly grubby labyrinth is popular with slumming minor celebrities and ex-backpackers. Some rooms are real gems – spacious and atmospheric – while others are small and junky. All of them share bathrooms. It's always packed; take what you can get.
✉ 225 E 17th St btw 2nd & 3rd Aves ☎ 475-2845 fax 677-8178 e www.hotel17 .citysearch.com 🚇 Union Sq

Hotel Wolcott (3, B5)

The rooms don't live up to the fancy beaux arts marble-and-mirrors lobby,

but they're spacious and not bad for the price, especially if you're sharing (some of the rooms can accommodate four). TVs come with attached games consoles.
✉ 4 W 31st St at 5th Ave ☎ 268-2900 fax 563-0096 e www .wolcott.com 🚇 33rd St, 34th St-Herald Sq

Lil's Guest House

(3, F9) Though there are only seven rooms in this appealing guesthouse, they're all light, spacious and pleasant. Everyone will appreciate the home comforts and low prices, but the private bathrooms, fully equipped kitchens and kid-friendly management make this an especially great choice for families. Weekly rates are available.
✉ 270 E 7th St btw Aves C & D ☎ 777-5270 fax 777-5270 🚇 1st Ave, Delancey-Essex Sts

Madison Hotel (3, C5)

This gruff but well-meaning hotel veers between colorful and depressing. Rooms range from 'cozy' to spacious (if a little dim), and the bathrooms are adequate but tubless. The price is right, though, especially January through March, when double rooms drop to $88.
✉ 21 E 27th St at Madison Ave ☎ 532-7373 fax 686-0092 e www.madison-hotel .com 🚇 28th St

facts for the visitor

Angus Oborn

Central Park and beyond

ARRIVAL & DEPARTURE

New York is readily accessible from most places in the world and from within the USA. There are direct flights from London, Dublin, Paris and other European cities and from Mexico and Central and South American cities. Flights from Australia and New Zealand stop in San Francisco or Los Angeles. Many flights from Asian destinations like Japan and China make connections in Honolulu.

Air

Three international airports serve New York; the Air Ride line (☎ 800-247-7433) offers information on transportation to/from all of them.

JFK International Airport

The John F Kennedy International Airport (4, C5), in southeastern Queens, is about 15 miles (24km) away from Midtown, or 45-75mins by car.

Left Luggage
Facilities at Terminals 1 and 4 charge approximately $5/bag.

Information
General Inquiries & Flight Information
☎ 718-244-4444

Parking Information
☎ 718-244-4444

Hotel Booking Service
☎ 267-5500

Airport Access
Bus The New York Airport Service (☎ 875-8200) buses run every 15-20mins 5am-midnight, stopping at 125 Park Ave btw 41st & 42nd Sts (2, O7); the Port Authority Bus Terminal (2, O4); Penn Station (2, P4) and Midtown hotels. Allow 60-75mins for the trip. You'll pay $13/person.

Taxi The fare to Manhattan is a flat $30 plus tolls and tip. The flat fare rate is not available outbound to the airport.

Shared Ride Expect to pay about $15/person; contact SuperShuttle (☎ 258-3826).

Car Service Expect to pay around $50. Contact Big Apple (☎ 718-232-1015), Dial (☎ 718-743-2877) or Citywide (☎ 718-405-5822).

Subway The train ride to the Howard Beach-JFK station takes around 1hr from Midtown. Take the A train marked Far Rockaway or Rockaway Park to Howard Beach-JFK, then catch the Long Term Parking Bus to the terminals.

Some time in 2002, the JFK Airtrain will connect Howard Beach to each terminal. Beginning in 2003, the Airtrain will also connect with the E, J and Z subway trains in Jamaica, Queens.

La Guardia Airport

La Guardia (6, B3) is in northern Queens, about 8 miles (13km) from Midtown, or 20-45mins by car.

Left Luggage
There are no left-luggage facilities.

Information
General Inquiries & Flight Information
☎ 718-533-3400

Parking Information
☎ 718-533-3400

Hotel Booking Service
☎ 267-5500

Airport Access
Bus From the airport, take the M60 bus to W 106th St & Broadway in Manhattan, or use the New York

Airport Service (☎ 875-8200); buses leave every 20mins 6am-midnight. The ride ($11) takes about 30mins.

Taxi The fare to/from Midtown is around $25 plus tolls and tips.

Shared Ride SuperShuttle (☎ 258-3826) charges about $14/person.

Car Service Expect to pay around $30 plus tolls and tips. Contact the companies listed in the JFK airport section.

Newark International Airport

Situated in New Jersey, 10 miles (16km) west of Manhattan, Newark (4, E1) is a 30-60min drive from Midtown Manhattan.

Left Luggage

There are no left-luggage facilities.

Information

General Inquiries & Flight Information
☎ 973-961-6000

Parking Information
☎ 973-961-6000

Hotel Booking Service
☎ 267-5500

Airport Access

Train Take NJ Transit from Penn Station to the new Newark International Airport station. The ride costs $11.15. Alternatively, take the cheaper PATH train ($1.50) to Newark Penn Station, then the Airlink bus to the airport.

Bus Take Olympia Trails (☎ 964-6233) from the Port Authority Bus Terminal (2, O4), Penn Station (2, P4) and Grand Central Terminal (2, N7); the fare is $11.

Taxi The fare to/from Midtown is about $45 plus $10 for tolls.

Shared Ride SuperShuttle (☎ 258-3826) charges about $19/person.

Car Service Fees start around $55. See the companies listed in the JFK airport section.

Bus

Long-distance and commuter buses arrive at and depart from the Port Authority Bus Terminal (41st St at 8th Ave; 2, O4; ☎ 564-8484), near Times Square.

Train

Long-distance trains (Amtrak) arrive at and depart from Pennsylvania (Penn) Station (33rd St at 8th Ave; 2, P4; ☎ 582-6875 or 800-872-7245). Commuter trains (MetroNorth) use Grand Central Terminal (Park Ave at 42nd St; 2, N7; ☎ 532-4900). New Jersey PATH (Port Authority Trans-Hudson) trains (☎ 800-234-7284) stop at several stations in downtown Manhattan.

Travel Documents

Passport

All foreigners except Canadians need a passport that's valid for at least six months after their planned stay in the USA. Canadians need proof of citizenship with photo ID.

Visa

Visas are generally not required for most visitors. Citizens of Australia, New Zealand, Ireland, the UK and some other countries may enter for 90 days or fewer without a visa. Everyone not covered by the visa waiver exemption and those wishing to stay longer need to get a visa from a US consulate or embassy.

Return/Onward Ticket

To enter, you must have a return ticket that's nonrefundable in the US.

Customs

If you're carrying more than $10,000 in US and/or foreign cash, traveler's checks or money orders when you enter the US, you must declare it.

Duty Free

You can import 1L of liquor (if you are over the age of 21); 100 cigars (provided they are not Cuban), 200 cigarettes or 2kg of tobacco; and gifts up to a total value of $100 ($400 for US citizens).

Departure Tax

There are no separate departure charges to leave a US airport. Any airport charges are included in the price of your air ticket.

GETTING AROUND

Most of Manhattan's grid system is packed with traffic during the day (a phenomenon known as 'gridlock'). The subway is generally the fastest, cheapest way to get around. City buses can be useful if you are traveling north-south, provided that traffic is moving. Pick up a public transit map from subway ticket booths. Taxis are the most convenient mode of transportation after 10pm.

Travel Passes

MetroCard (☎ 638-7622) is the easiest way to pay for travel on New York's public transit system. Regular cards are available for $3 and up. Spend $15 and get a $1.50 bonus; spend $20 for a $2 bonus; spend $30 for a $3 bonus (that's two free rides!). A one-day unlimited-ride card is $4; a 7-day card is $17. You can transfer between buses and subways within a 2hr period when using the MetroCard system.

Subway

The subway system (☎ 718-330-1234) runs 24hrs/day over 25 different routes linking 468 stations. If you're traveling by subway, be aware that the terrorist attacks on September 11, 2001, damaged several stations in Lower Manhattan and resulted in limited service on certain lines, so call ahead or visit the MTA website (**e** www.mta .info) for travel advisories or advice about alternate routes.

If you are not using MetroCard, you can buy single-use tokens ($1.50) from station booths.

In this book, our subway listings note the nearest stop's name (followed by the line number or letter in parentheses in cases where two different stations have the same name).

Bus

City buses (☎ 718-330-1234) operate 24hrs/day and generally run north-south along avenues and crosstown along the major east-west thoroughfares. You need a MetroCard, exact change of $1.50 or a token to board a bus.

Names of bus routes that begin and end in Manhattan start with M (eg, M5); Queens bus routes start with Q, Brooklyn with B, and the Bronx with Bx. Some 'Limited Stop' buses pull over only every 10 blocks or so, but at night you can ask to be let off at any point along the route. 'Express' buses ($3) are primarily for outer-borough commuters, not for people taking short trips.

Train

New Jersey PATH trains (☎ 800-234-7284; @ www.pathrail.com) run down 6th Ave to Jersey City and Newark, with stops at 33rd, 23rd, 14th, 9th and Christopher Sts in Manhattan. These reliable trains run every 15mins 24hrs/day. The fare is $1.50, and machines accept coins and $1 and $5 bills.

Prior to September 11, 2001, a PATH line went from northern New Jersey to the World Trade Center. Call for information about the potential resumption of service to Lower Manhattan.

Boat

NY Waterway (☎ 800-533-3779) ferries make runs up the Hudson River Valley and from Midtown out to Yankee Stadium (4, A2) in the Bronx. A popular commuter route goes from the New Jersey Transit train station in Hoboken (4, C2) to a pier in Lower Manhattan; at press time, the company was planning to relocate from its original spot at the World Financial Center to Pier A in Battery Park, a little farther away from the site of the terrorist attacks. Boats leave every 5-10mins at peak times, and the 10min ride costs $2 each way.

Taxi

Taxis are available whenever the rooftop license number is alight (as opposed to the 'off duty' side lights). Fares are metered and start at $2; tip 10-15% (minimum 50¢). There's a 50¢ surcharge 8pm-6am. For trips longer than 50 blocks, instruct the driver to take a road well away from Midtown traffic.

Be careful not to take a ride in an unlicensed taxi, which carries a greater risk of accidents.

Limousine

Limousines and car services can be an affordable way to travel, especially for groups. Affordable Limousine Service (☎ 888-338-4567) and Carmel (☎ 666-6666) charge about $30/hr for one to four people; a night on the town for eight costs $120 (3hrs).

Car & Motorcycle

Traffic congestion, the high incidence of car theft and the expense of parking and gas more than offset any convenience afforded by having a car here. Plus, you'll spend 15mins finding a parking spot and 15mins walking to your destination; save time by opting for public transportation. Some attractions reserve parking spots for disabled drivers – call ahead to check. Disabled parking permits are only available to New York residents. (If you don't have a permit, never park in spaces reserved for the disabled; fines are very high.)

Road Rules

Drive on the right hand side of the road. Turn right at a red light only if a sign specifically permits it, and don't block intersections – the wrath of other drivers is worse than the stiff penalties you might incur. All front-seat occupants must wear seat belts; all back-seat occupants under the age of 10 must wear seat belts or other suitable restraints.

Driving while your ability is impaired by drugs or alcohol is forbidden; specifically, driving with a blood alcohol level of .05 (.02 if you're under 21) or above is against the law. The state maximum speed limit is 55mph (just over 70km/h); however, you will need to watch for lower limits on city streets and in school zones.

Rental

Car rental rates are expensive, and cheaper deals at the airport are rare. Make arrangements for some sort of a package deal before you arrive.

Among the main rental agencies are Avis (☎ 800-331-1212), Budget (☎ 800-527-0700), Dollar (☎ 800-800-4000), Hertz (☎ 800-654-3131) and Thrifty (☎ 800-367-2277).

Driver's License

If you intend to drive, you will need a license from your home country.

Motoring Organizations

If you're doing a lot of driving, think about joining the American Automobile Association (AAA; ☎ 757-2000), a national automobile club that offers emergency road service (☎ 800-AAA-HELP), maps and even travel assistance. Membership may entitle you to reduced hotel rates.

Bicycle

Rent bikes from Hub Station (517 Broome St; 3, J5; ☎ 965-9334) for around $25/day.

PRACTICAL INFORMATION

Climate & When to Go

There are always *lots* of tourists in New York City, although numbers decline slightly in January and February. The most pleasant and temperate times to visit are May, early June and mid-September to October (but expect hotel prices to be high). Wet weather is common in November and April. Snow typically falls from December to February. High average temperatures and humidity, together with poor air quality, can make summer in New York an uncomfortable experience. Most hotels, restaurants and shops are air-conditioned.

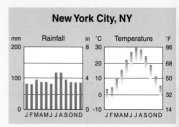

New York City, NY

Tourist Information

Tourist Information Abroad

NYC & Co, the local tourist board, maintains offices in London (33-34 Carnaby St, London WIF 7DW; ☎ 207-437-8300) and in Munich (Herzogspitalstrasse 5, D-80331 Munich; ☎ 89-236-6210).

Local Tourist Information

NYC & Co (810 7th Ave at 53rd St; 2, M5; ☎ 484-1222; [e] www.nyc

visit.com) operates a 24hr toll-free line that provides listings of special events and reservation details. Staff at the comprehensive information center are knowledgeable and helpful; it's open weekdays 8:30am-6pm and weekends 9am-5pm.

You'll also find information counters and centers at airports, in Times Square (2, N5), at Grand Central Terminal (2, N7) and at Penn Station (2, P4). The Big Apple Greeters Program (1 Centre St; 3, L6; ☎ 669-8159; [e] www.bigapplegreeter.org) organizes volunteers to introduce visitors to the city for free.

The New York State Travel Information Center (Empire State Plaza, Main Concourse, Room 110,

Albany, NY 12220; ☎ 800-225-5697; e www.iloveny.state.ny.us) can provide ideas for recreation and holidays in New York State.

For other sources of information, see Newspapers & Magazines (p. 118) and Useful Sites under Email/www (p. 118).

Embassies & Consulates

The UN's presence in New York means that nearly every country in the world maintains diplomatic offices here. Most are listed in the white pages of the phone book under 'Consulates General of (country).' Some embassies in Manhattan include:

Australia
   (2, O7; ☎ 351-6500) 150 E 42nd St btw
   Lexington & 3rd Aves

Canada
   (2, M5; ☎ 596-1783) 1251 6th Ave btw
   49th & 50th Sts

Ireland
   (2, M7; ☎ 319-2555) 345 Park Ave btw
   51st & 52nd Sts

New Zealand
   (2, M7; ☎ 832-4038) 780 3rd Ave btw
   48th & 49th Sts

South Africa
   (2, O8; ☎ 213-4880) 333 E 38th St btw
   1st & 2nd Aves

UK
   (2, M7; ☎ 745-0202) 845 3rd Ave btw
   51st & 52nd Sts

Money

Currency

The monetary unit used is the US dollar, which is divided into 100 cents (¢). Coins come in 1¢ (penny), 5¢ (nickel), 10¢ (dime), 25¢ (quarter), 50¢ (half-dollar; rare) and $1 denominations. Notes come in $1, $2 (rare), $5, $10, $20, $50 and $100. Some shops won't accept notes in denominations higher than $20.

Traveler's Checks

Checks issued by American Express (☎ 800-221-7282) and Thomas Cook (☎ 800-287-7362) are widely accepted and can be easily replaced if stolen or lost. Restaurants, hotels and most stores readily accept US-dollar traveler's checks. Fast-food restaurants and smaller businesses sometimes refuse to accept checks.

Credit Cards

Visa, MasterCard (both affiliated with European Access Cards) and American Express are widely accepted, Discover and Diners Club less so. For lost cards, contact:

American Express	☎ 800-992-3404
Diners Club	☎ 800-234-6377
Discover	☎ 800-347-2683
MasterCard	☎ 800-826-2181
Visa	☎ 800-336-8472

ATMs

You'll find thousands of 24hr ATMs at banks; most grocery stores also have machines. Citibank doesn't charge non-US cardholders a fee to withdraw cash from its ATMs.

Changing Money

Banks often offer better deals than exchange offices. Always check the rates, commissions and any other charges. Chase, a bank with 80 branches in Manhattan, doesn't charge fees.

Banks are open weekdays 9am-5pm. Several banks along Canal St in Chinatown are open weekends.

Tipping

Tips are rarely included as a service charge on a hotel or restaurant bill and must be given separately. Many restaurants add a 15-20% 'tip' to the bill for groups of six or more – be sure to look out for that so you don't tip twice.

Use the following chart to figure out how much to give:

Baggage carriers – $1 for the first bag, 50¢ for each additional bag

Bars – at least $1 per drink (more if you want faster service and stronger drinks next time you order)

Cloakroom attendants – $1 per item

Doormen, bellboys, parking attendants – $1 for each service performed (eg, opening a taxi door)

Hairdressers – 15%

Restaurants – 15-20% (not expected in fast-food, takeout or self-service restaurants)

Room cleaners – up to $5 per day

Taxis – 10%

Tour guides – $5 per family/group for a full-day tour

Discounts

Students, children (under 12) and seniors get discounts at most attractions and on most forms of transportation. Many attractions also offer reduced-price tickets for families. Students must present university IDs for discounts. Seniors can also expect cut rates on hotel charges, drugstore (pharmacy) prescriptions and cinema prices.

See p. 12 for information about CityPass.

Travel Insurance

A policy covering theft, loss, medical expenses and compensation for sudden cancellation or delays in your travel arrangements is highly recommended. If items are lost or stolen, make sure you get a police report right away – otherwise your insurer might not pay up.

Opening Hours

Office hours are weekdays 9am-5pm. Shops are open Monday to Saturday 10am-6pm and Sunday noon-6pm. Museums and art galleries are typically open Tuesday to Sunday 10am-5pm. On public holidays, banks, schools and government offices (including post offices) are closed, and transportation ser-vices run on a Sunday schedule.

Public Holidays

Jan 1	New Year's Day
3rd Mon in Jan	Martin Luther King Jr Day
3rd Mon in Feb	Presidents' Day
Mar/Apr	Easter Sunday
Last Mon in May	Memorial Day
Jul 4	Independence Day
1st Mon in Sep	Labor Day
2nd Mon in Oct	Columbus Day
Nov 11	Veterans' Day
4th Thurs in Nov	Thanksgiving Day
Dec 25	Christmas Day

Time

New York is in the Eastern Standard Time (EST) zone, which is 5hrs behind Greenwich Mean Time (GMT). Daylight-saving starts on the first Sunday in April, when the clocks are advanced 1hr; it finishes on the last Saturday in October. At noon in New York City, it's:

9am in San Francisco
5pm in London
6pm in Paris
7pm in Cape Town
3am (following day) in Sydney

Electricity

Electricity in the USA is 110V and 60Hz. Plugs have two or three pins (two flat pins, often with a round 'grounding' pin). Adapters for European and South American plugs are widely available; Australians should bring adapters.

Weights & Measures

Americans hate the metric system and continue to resist it. Distances are in feet, yards and miles. Dry weights are measured by the ounce, pound and ton; liquid measures differ from dry measures. Gasoline is dispensed by the US gallon (about 20% less than the imperial gallon). US pints and quarts are also 20% less than imperial ones. See p. 122 for a Conversion Table.

Post

Postal Rates

Domestic/international rates are 34¢/60¢ for letters, 21¢/55¢ for postcards. Stamps are available from post office counters and vending machines. Buying them from hotel concierges and souvenir stores costs 25% more.

Opening Hours

The main post office (421 8th Ave at 33rd St; 2, P4; ☎ 967-8585) is open 24hrs. The Rockefeller Center post office (2, M5) is open weekdays 9:30am-5:30pm. The Franklin D Roosevelt post office (909 3rd Ave; 2, M7) is open weekdays 9am-8pm and Saturday 10am-2pm. Other branches are listed in the Government Listings section of the white pages in the phone directory.

Telephone

Public phones are either coin- or card-operated; some accept credit cards. Use a major carrier such as AT&T (☎ 800-321-0288) for long-distance calls.

Phone Cards

Newsstands and pharmacies sell prepaid phone cards, but they can be huge rip-offs, charging rates a lot higher than those promised. Lonely Planet's eKno Communication Card, specifically aimed at travelers, provides competitive rates for international calls (avoid using it for local calls), messaging services and free email. Go to e www.ekno.com.

Mobile Phones

The US uses the GSM system – you'll need a GSM-compatible phone to make and receive calls here. See Doing Business (p. 118) for rental information.

Country & City Area Codes

The US country code is 1. Manhattan land lines have two area codes: ☎ 212 and the new ☎ 646. In this book, all numbers start with ☎ 212 unless otherwise noted. If you're dialing another area code, even if both numbers are within Manhattan, you must dial ☎ 1, the area code and the seven-digit number. For the four outer boroughs, the area codes are ☎ 718 and ☎ 347. Pager and cell numbers (and a few land lines) begin with ☎ 917.

Useful Numbers

Directory Assistance	☎ 411
International Dialing Code	☎ 011
Operator	☎ 0
Operator-Assisted Calls (+ the number; an operator will come on after you have dialed)	☎ 01
Collect (Reverse-Charge)	☎ 0
Time	☎ 976-1616
Weather	☎ 976-1212
Moviefone	☎ 777-3456
Clubfone	☎ 777-2582

International Codes

Dial ☎ 00 followed by:

Australia	☎ 61
Canada	☎ 1
Japan	☎ 81
New Zealand	☎ 64
South Africa	☎ 27
UK	☎ 44

Email/www

Public libraries offer free Internet access, and Internet cafés are common throughout New York.

Internet Service Providers

Major national ISPs include AOL (dial-in: ☎ 871-1021) and AT&T (dial-in: ☎ 824-2405).

Internet Cafés

If you can't access the Internet from where you're staying, head to one of these cybercafés:

Cybercafe
(3, H6; ☎ 334-5140) 273 Lafayette St at Prince St; (2, M4) 250 W 49th St btw Broadway & 8th Ave; e www.cyber-cafe.com; Mon-Fri 8.30am-10pm, Sat-Sun 11am-10pm; $12.80/hr

easyInternetCafé
(2, O5; ☎ 398-0775) W 42nd St btw 7th & 8th Aves; e www.easyeverything .com; 24hrs; prices vary

Internet Cafe
(3, G7; ☎ 614-0747) 82 E 3rd St, btw 1st & 2nd Aves; e www.bigmagic.com; Mon-Sat 11am-2am, Sun 11am-midnight; $10/hr

Useful Sites

Lonely Planet's very own website (e www.lonelyplanet.com) offers New York City information and links. Other good sites include:

New York City Search
e www.newyork.citysearch.com

New York Times
e www.nytimes.com

NYC & Co
e www.nycvisit.com

New York City Insider
e www.theinsider.com

New York 1 News
e www.ny1.com

New York City's official site
e www.nyc.gov

Doing Business

All top-end hotels have business centers with computers, dataports, fax machines and administrative staff. Some hotels rent space in these centers to nonguests.

US Rental.Com (☎ 594-2222) rents PC and Mac desktops and laptops for approximately $100/week or $200/month (delivery, pick-up and onsite servicing included).

Access World Wireless Services (☎ 800-840-6051) and International Cellular Services (☎ 800-897-5788) offer cell phone rental. Their expensive rates include delivery.

Unique Support Services (☎ 406-0062) rents out administrative assistants by the day or half-day. Rates for basic word-processing start at $25/hr.

If you need foreign-language expertise, Berlitz Translation Services (☎ 917-339-4700) translates documents and provides interpreters for business meetings and conferences.

Newspapers & Magazines

The New York Times is the nation's premier newspaper; its Weekend section, published Friday, is an invaluable guide to cultural events. The New York Observer specializes in local media and politics. The Daily News and New York Post are popular tabloids. The Wall Street Journal is the daily business bible.

Time Out New York lists events, restaurants and shops; the New Yorker magazine covers high-brow theater, art and music events. Free street papers – the Village Voice and New York Press are the best known – offer good entertainment listings. Where New York (available in hotels) is the best free monthly guide to mainstream events and museums.

Radio

WBAI (99.5FM) is an interesting independent station; WINS (1010AM) offers continuous weather and news. WNYC (880AM) is the New York branch of the excellent National Public Radio network, and WNYU (89.1FM) is a local college station.

TV

The four major broadcast networks (NBC, CBS, ABC and FOX) offer familiar prime-time fare; alternatives are the local New York 1 and the Public Broadcasting Service (PBS). Cable carries well-known networks like CNN, MTV and HBO.

Photography & Video

Print film is widely available at supermarkets and discount drugstores; 35mm slide film is harder to find. Camera shops stock B&W film. If you purchase a video, note that the USA uses NTSC color TV standard, which is not compatible with the other standards (PAL or SECAM) used elsewhere.

Health

Immunizations
No immunizations are required to enter the US.

Precautions
New York tap water is safe to drink; nonetheless, many residents drink bottled or filtered water. Encephalitis outbreaks sometimes prompt citywide spraying and advice that residents should wear long sleeves and mosquito repellent, but generally New York is as healthy as other big, dirty cities.

Practice the usual precautions when it comes to sex; condoms are available from drugstores and nightclub vending machines.

Insurance & Medical Treatment

Definitely have medical insurance when you enter the USA, as medical care is extremely expensive. Doctors often expect payment on the spot for services rendered. Sometimes you'll have to pay up front, and your insurance company will reimburse you.

New York Hotel Urgent Medical Services (☎ 737-1212) offers medical services, including dental and homeopathic care, to visitors; doctors make 24hr house (and hotel) calls. Prices start at $200, including most medication.

Medical Services
If you have a medical emergency, call ☎ 911. Hospitals with 24hr emergency departments include:

Bellevue Hospital
(3, C7; ☎ 562-4141) 1st Ave at E 27th St

Lenox Hill Hospital
(2, G7; ☎ 434-2000) 100 E 77th St btw Park & Lexington Aves

New York Hospital
(2, J9; ☎ 746-5050) 525 E 68th St btw York Ave & Franklin D Roosevelt Dr

Dental Services
The Stuyvesant Dentist Association (430 E 20th St at 1st Ave; 3, D7; ☎ 473-4151) can help with pediatric and general dental issues.

Pharmacies
Among the 24hr pharmacies are:

Duane Reade
(2, L4; ☎ 541-9708) W 57th St at Broadway

Duane Reade
(3, G4; ☎ 674-5357) 6th Ave near Waverly Pl

Genovese
(2, J8; ☎ 772-0104) 1299 2nd Ave at 68th St

Toilets

Public toilets are rare, and most businesses provide facilities for customers only. If you're in distress, head to a department store or a fast-food restaurant.

A word of advice for international visitors: ask for the 'bathroom' or the 'restroom' when you want to find out where the loo is. Major attractions and large restaurants tend to have accessible toilet facilities for the disabled, but many smaller restaurants and bars don't.

Safety Concerns

As everywhere else, it's wise to keep your money and valuables hidden and secure. Panhandlers and hustlers can target tourists, but don't feel obligated to give money. If you'd like to find another way to help New Yorkers in need, volunteer for a short project at New York Cares (☎ 228-5000).

Many streets in New York stay lively till the wee hours and are no more dangerous at night than they are by day. Generally, avoid badly lit or deserted places. Central Park, often best avoided at night, is quite safe when there's a concert or a play at the Delacorte Theater.

Lost Property

If you lose something on public transit, call ☎ 712-4500. For items lost in taxis, call ☎ 692-8294.

Keeping Copies

Make photocopies of important documents and keep some with you (separate from the originals), but always leave a copy at home. You can also store details of documents in Lonely Planet's free online Travel Vault, password-protected and accessible worldwide. Visit the website at e www.ekno.com.

Emergency Numbers

Police, Fire, Ambulance ☎ 911
Police Information Operator ☎ 374-5000

Women Travelers

Women need not be particularly concerned about traveling on their own in New York City. Many shun the subways, but in reality the transit system boasts a lower crime rate than the city streets. At night, you might consider riding in the conductor's car (in the middle of the train). If someone stares or acts in an annoying manner, simply move to another part of the car or near the conductor's booth. On the street, men might make harassing comments, but most will take their obnoxious behavior no further if you ignore them and walk on.

Tampons and pads are widely available, though there's a smaller selection of tampons in the US than in Europe or Australia. The contraceptive pill and 'morning after' pill are available by prescription only.

Gay & Lesbian Travelers

New York is one of the most gay-friendly cities on earth, and several city neighborhoods – particularly Greenwich Village and Chelsea in Manhattan and Jackson Heights in Queens – are populated by many gays and lesbians.

Information & Organizations

The free magazines *HX* and *Next* are available at restaurants and bars. Look for *LGNY* and *NY Blade* in street-corner boxes. Pick up the lifestyle magazine *Metrosource* at shops and at the Lesbian & Gay Community Services Center (see address, next page). *Time Out New York* features a good events section.

Useful counseling, referral and information centers include:

Gay & Lesbian Hotline
(☎ 989-0999) ⓔ glnh@glnh.org

Lesbian & Gay Community Services Center
(3, G3; ☎ 620-7310) 208 W 13th St;
ⓔ www.gaycenter.org

Senior Travelers

New Yorkers tend to be respectful toward older people – if you're a senior, you'll usually be offered a seat on public transportation, at the very least.

Information & Organizations
The American Association of Retired Persons (AARP; PO Box 199, Long Beach, CA 90801; ☎ 800-424-3410; ⓔ www.aarp.org) offers hotel and car rental discounts (10-50%) to those over 50. Membership costs $10/year.

The mayor's Senior Action Line office (☎ 788-7504) is staffed by volunteers weekdays 11am-1pm.

Disabled Travelers

Federal laws require that all government offices offer elevator and ramp access for wheelchairs, plus devices to aid the hearing-impaired. Almost all major venues have good bathroom facilities for those with wheelchairs, and all city buses are able to carry wheelchair passengers. Only some subway stations are accessible (call ☎ 718-596-8585). In this guidebook, the wheelchair-accessible attractions are noted with ♿.

Information & Organizations
The book *Access for All* is a disabled guide to New York attractions. To get a copy, contact Hospital Audiences (548 Broadway, New York, NY 10012; ☎ 575-7676; ⓔ www .hospitalaudiences.org).

Helpful contacts include:

Big Apple Greeters
☎ 669-8159

New York Society for the Deaf
☎ 777-3900

People with Disabilities Office
☎ 788-2830, TTY ☎ 788-2838

Public Transport Accessible Line
☎ 718-596-8585,
TTY ☎ 800-734-7433

Society for Accessible Travel and Hospitality (SATH)
☎ 447-7284; ⓔ www.sath.org

State Commission for the Blind
☎ 961-4450

Language

New Yorkers have added a lot to the American idiom. US English has borrowed countless words from the languages of successive waves of immigrants who made New York City their point of arrival. From Germans have come words like 'hoodlum,' from Yiddish-speaking Jews words like 'schmuck' (a fool), and from the Irish words like 'galore.' Today's large Hispanic population has made Spanish a semiofficial second language. A popular Spanish-English hybrid has not yet evolved, but it's on its way: everyone knows that 'bodega' is slang for 'convenience store.'

Songs of the streets

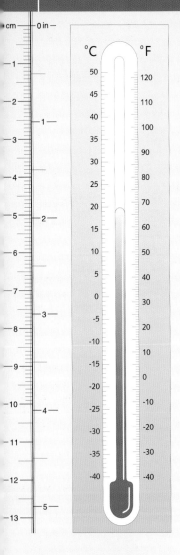

Conversion Table

Clothing Sizes
Measurements approximate only; try before you buy.

Women's Clothing

Aust/NZ	8	10	12	14	16	18
Europe	36	38	40	42	44	46
Japan	5	7	9	11	13	15
UK	8	10	12	14	16	18
USA	6	8	10	12	14	16

Women's Shoes

Aust/NZ	5	6	7	8	9	10
Europe	35	36	37	38	39	40
France only	35	36	38	39	40	42
Japan	22	23	24	25	26	27
UK	3fi	4fi	5fi	6fi	7fi	8fi
USA	5	6	7	8	9	10

Men's Clothing

Aust/NZ	92	96	100	104	108	112
Europe	46	48	50	52	54	56
Japan	S		M	M		L
UK	35	36	37	38	39	40
USA	35	36	37	38	39	40

Men's Shirts (Collar Sizes)

Aust/NZ	38	39	40	41	42	43
Europe	38	39	40	41	42	43
Japan	38	39	40	41	42	43
UK	15	15fi	16	16fi	17	17fi
USA	15	15fi	16	16fi	17	17fi

Men's Shoes

Aust/NZ	7	8	9	10	11	12
Europe	41	42	43	44fi	46	47
Japan	26	27	27.5	28	29	30
UK	7	8	9	10	11	12
USA	7fi	8fi	9fi	10fi	11fi	12fi

Weights & Measures

Weight
1kg = 2.2lb
1lb = 0.45kg
1g = 0.04oz
1oz = 28g

Volume
1 litre = 0.26 US gallons
1 US gallon = 3.8 litres
1 litre = 0.22 imperial gallons
1 imperial gallon = 4.55 litres

Length & Distance
1 inch = 2.54cm
1cm = 0.39 inches
1m = 3.3ft = 1.1yds
1ft = 0.3m
1km = 0.62 miles
1 mile = 1.6km

lonely planet

Lonely Planet is the world's most successful independent travel information company, with offices in Australia, the US, UK and France. With a reputation for comprehensive, reliable travel information, Lonely Planet is a print and electronic publishing leader, with over 650 titles and 22 series catering to travelers' individual needs.

At Lonely Planet we believe that travelers can make a positive contribution to the countries they visit – if they respect their host communities and spend their money wisely. Since 1986 a percentage of the income from books has been donated to aid human-rights projects.

www.lonelyplanet.com

For news, views and free subscriptions to print and email newsletters, and a full list of Lonely Planet titles, click on our award-winning website.

On the Town

A romantic escape to Paris or a mad shopping dash through New York City, the locals' secret bars or a city's top attractions – whether you have 24 hours to kill or months to explore, Lonely Planet's On the Town products will give you the low-down.

Condensed guides are ideal pocket guides for when time is tight. Their quick-view maps, full-color layout and opinionated reviews help short-term visitors target the top sights and discover the very best eating, shopping and entertainment options a city has to offer.

For more in-depth coverage, **City guides** offer insights into a city's character and cultural background, as well as providing broad coverage of where to eat, stay and play. **CitySync**, a digital guide for your handheld unit, allows you to reference stacks of opinionated, well-researched travel information. Portable and durable **City Maps** are perfect for locating those backstreet bars or hard-to-find local haunts.

'Ideal for a generation of fast movers.'

– *Gourmet Traveller* on Condensed guides

Condensed Guides

- Amsterdam
- Athens (May 2002)
- Barcelona (May 2002)
- Boston
- California
- Chicago

- Crete
- Dublin
- Frankfurt
- Hong Kong
- London
- New York City
- Paris

- Prague (May 2002)
- Rome
- Sydney
- Tokyo
- Venice (June 2002)
- Washington, DC (May 2002)

index

See also separate indexes for Places to Eat (p. 126), Places to Stay (p. 126), Shops (p. 127) and Sights with map references (p. 128).

PLACES TO STAY

PLACES TO EAT

SHOPS

sights – quick index